Faith and

of the B. ethren

What They Are and

Why They Matter

ALEXANDER KURIAN

ISBN:9781073400096

TO MY BELOVED WIFE VALSA KURIAN

who belongs to the fourth generation of a noble family within the Brethren Movement in Kerala, India. She has been a faithful companion along the way, sacrificially supporting me and exemplifying the true Brethren ideals of life and ministry. "Her children rise up and call her blessed; her husband also, and he praises her."

Table of Contents

Acknowledgments

I would like to express my deep gratitude to my dear friend and brother in the Lord, Mr. Raymond Johnson, for his personal kindness and professional expertise in the publication of this book. My son Alex Kurian, Jr., and my daughter Shelley Kurian, helped me to see several matters discussed in this book from the perspective of the younger generation. Our lively discussions on the topics in the book were educational and enlightening. Thank you.

Most of the contents of this book have been published in 2014 by FIBA (Fellowship of the Indian Brethren families in North America) under the title *This We Believe*. It was a very timely project. Thanks to FIBA. But the present volume is revised, expanded, and modified with a new title.

I am grateful to God for all of you brothers and sisters who pray for me and encourage me in the great work of the Gospel.

Above all, with profound gratitude to my Lord and Savior Jesus Christ, who called me to the privilege of serving Him from a very young age and graciously equipped my life for the task. I pray that my Lord Jesus Christ will receive glory through this book as it is used to grow His church.

Why This Book?

"Fight the good fight of faith" (1 Tim.6:12)

This book has been shaped through my own study of the Scriptures and Brethren history. My continued exposure and association with the Brethren around the world has helped me to think through the issues presented here and evaluate them **scripturally** and **practically**. Other books written on the same subject deal primarily with a doctrinal emphasis with no historical or practical insights evaluating the beliefs and practices of the Brethren. Applying the biblical truths practically and effectively is more important than just a statement of doctrine as a creed. It is also important to evaluate whether we have correctly implemented the so-called distinctives in accordance with scriptural guidelines? Have we succeeded in this? Don't we feel the need for a sober reflection on the validity of our claims?

It is the practice of biblical truths that should concern us the most and that is the burden and vision carried in this book. The need to understand doctrine correctly, to implement it graciously, to witness to it effectively, and to evaluate it scripturally, is the way we should approach our distinctives. I believe there is a great need to set forth clearly *where we came from, who we are, what we believe, and why we believe what we believe.* I consider what we believe and practice to be of great significance and relevance because of its crucial importance to biblical, historical, pastoral, practical, and theological issues.

I was convinced for the last several years that there is an increasing need to know our faith from a clear biblical perspective, and to distinguish it from the so-called "Brethren traditions" (or "Brethrenism," Brethren denominationalism/sectarianism etc.), which sometimes is legalistically added to the faith and interpreted, presented, and practiced as doctrine. I have seen this happening all over the world among the Brethren. Many *traditions* (some of them good, healthy, and noble) have become biblical *absolutes.* Many assemblies have succumbed to this trap in different shapes and forms. Growing up in India, I was under the impression that this is a problem restricted to Indian assemblies. In later years, to my surprise, I found that this is not so. This is a universal problem; a deceptive trap of the enemy to weaken our powerful testimony. Mixing of biblical truth with traditions, precedents, and preferences has caused a lot of confusion in the minds of many believers, especially in the young generation. Usually no clarification effort in this regard is carried out.

I believe the "distinctives" are to be well defined, systematically explained, convincingly taught, fine-tuned, and reevaluated in relation to its biblical basis, practice, and implementation. Hermeneutical integrity cannot be ignored in this process. Hence, this book is more than just a statement of the "distinctives" and differs from other books written on the same subject. I encourage you to use this book as a part of discussion and study in your assembly.

Have you wondered how some assemblies have lost its New Testament identity? In some places, one generation of believers have taken assembly matters to the "right extreme" without any biblical warrant to their position and practices. The next generation who has *endured* it for years, finally overreacted to it (or even rebelled against it), and have taken things to the "left extreme." To one group *nothing* goes; to the other *everything* goes! In this tug of war, many assemblies have lost their real identity and many others are in terrible decline. May God deliver us from the fatal failures of religion!

I believe, part of the problem we are facing in this generation is that we have lost a sense of history. The precious past is lost somewhere. Rudyard Kipling's poem entitled *"The Way through the Woods"* comes to mind:

"They shut the road through the woods

Seventy years ago

Weather and rain have undone it again

And now you would never know

There was once a road through the woods."

The **historical and theological roots** of the great spiritual awakening called the *Brethren Movement* are forgotten today. Hence, there is a great and legitimate need to rediscover the biblical heritage of the Brethren and their most cherished *distinctives*. We desperately need the spiritual dynamism and Christ-centered attitudes as exemplified in the spiritual revival that led to the Brethren Movement. This book is written to help us return to those truths that made the Brethren Movement spiritually great, vibrant, influential, and impacting. At the same time, it is a clarion call to make appropriate *changes* (not compromises) in relation to many of our practices, so that we may be able to minister effectively in a postmodern world.

What follows is by no means a history of the Brethren Movement. But it contains deep insights into the basic characteristics of this movement and its beliefs and practices. May God use it to enlighten, correct, challenge, change, encourage and instruct us for our own growth and edification, and then pass it along to others in love, humility, and grace.

As mentioned earlier, the aim here is more than just a statement of the distinctives. I have also explained the distinctives briefly, and tried to biblically defend them. Reasons for holding on to these distinctives are clearly brought out in the light of God's Word. I also have called attention to areas where we need to *redefine* these distinctives (that does not mean abandoning them), so that we can practice them more biblically and meaningfully with greater impact. The need to evaluate prayerfully how we practice these truths is also of paramount importance.

Let us all remember that there are areas of faith where we do not have to be dogmatic and inflexible. I believe the Brethren have to make appropriate changes (transformational) **urgently** in certain areas of our practice and ministry without biblical compromise. Failure to do this has considerably weakened our testimony in many parts of the world. The decline of the assemblies in many countries is a sad reminder of this hard truth. The proof is verifiable and undeniable. It is a FACT that deeply hurts. At the same time, God has mightily used His remnant for the glory of His name and for the extension of His Kingdom. The glowing testimony of the assemblies in many parts of the world, especially in Asia, Africa, and South America, attests to this fact.

I hope and pray that this book will serve as a record and a memorial of the most articulated *distinctives* of the Brethren to the coming generation. I feel humbled and at the same time privileged to be a part of this outstanding venture for the testimony of the truth of God's Word.

The deep sentiments of my own Brethren heritage are highly motivational for me to write this book. I was born and brought up in a Brethren home in Kerala, South India, though both my parents originally came from non-Brethren backgrounds, steeped in denominational ritualism and traditionalism. In their heroic and adventurous spiritual pilgrimage (a great story in itself), they embraced the "Brethren" fellowship as their own, out of conviction. For this they paid a very high price. Their unswerving commitment in life and ministry to the **simple** truths of the New Testament made an indelible impression on me. Their solid theology was not dead orthodoxy; it was an **art of living unto God**. That is why to this day I don't like the "dry brand of Brethren." I am ever grateful to God for that wonderful heritage rooted in *Sola Scriptura* (Scripture alone). I have not seen anything better so far.

Through a lifetime of association with the assemblies around the world, I came to know the Brethren well. I love them and call them "my people." My own sentiments and personal testimony in relation to the Brethren is reflected and superbly expressed by a very honorable Plymouth Brethren churchman of the last century –

F.F. Bruce (1910-1990), one of the most brilliant and influential biblical scholars of the twentieth century. This is what he had to say on staying with the Brethren all through his life:

"I have never found it a disadvantage to belong to the Brethren, and even if I did, that would be the worst possible reason for leaving them. I owe them an incalculable debt. It was among them that I learned my early lessons in the Christian way, and I hope I have been able in measure to repay that debt by passing on to others the lessons I have learned" (*In Retrospect,* Baker, 1993, *283).*

The subject of *distinctives* is a controversial one (and what subject is not?). It is not to be expected that all Brethren will agree with all that is presented here. In spite of its limitation and inadequacy, I trust that you will find the information helpful as you seek to understand the beliefs and practices of the Brethren. I want this to be a **brave** and **helpful** book to all who look for real renewal, and who are willing and courageous to make whatever changes may be needed. Its self-evaluative thrust is to lead the readers to the original vision of the early Brethren. My aim has been to make it **biblical, historical, practical, honest, realistic and relevant to our times.**

My appeal to the readers is to abandon a "tunnel vision" mentality, and to have "a big picture" before you as you move forward. I encourage you to approach and address the issues with openness, and with willingness to **change** whenever and wherever it is necessary. I believe you will join with me in my conviction that the best is yet to come for us. My prayer is that the information presented here will be useful to Brethren and non-Brethren alike.

Mistakes or errors of any kind belong to the ignorance and myopia of the author. Please forgive. Someone wrote to the godly Macarius of Optina (1788-1860) that his spiritual counsel had been helpful. "This cannot be," Macarius wrote in reply. "Only the mistakes are mine. All good advice is the advice of the Spirit of God; His advice I happen to have heard rightly and have passed on without distorting it."

"And of the sons of Issachar, men who understood the times, with knowledge of what Israel should do" (1Chro.12:32).

1

Our Legacy

"Buy the truth, and do not sell it" (Prov.23:23)

We have a great biblical heritage. The distinctives about which we always talk is solely based on the Scriptures. It is the fruit of the study of the Word.   A *distinctive* is a quality or characteristic that makes a person or thing different from others in a way that is easy to notice. It is a feature that helps to distinguish someone or something. *Distinctives of the Assemblies* is a reference to characteristic doctrines and practices that distinguish Christian assemblies generally known as "Christian Brethren", "Open Brethren" or "Plymouth Brethren" from other gatherings of Christians. The term *Assembly Distinctives* or *Brethren Distinctives* is **not** preferred by this writer as these *distinctives* are *not* the monopoly of the Brethren.   Other Christian congregations also practice these truths. The *distinctives* practiced by the Brethren are Scriptural truths and hence they are **biblical distinctives**.

If the *distinctives* are biblical, they are important and provide spiritual benefits to Christian life and ministry. The distinguishing features of the Christian assemblies are not derived from any

15

ecclesiastical traditions or denominational systems. We embrace them on the basis of Scriptural proof and support. Our position is **biblically defensible** (though at times the way we implement or practice them may not be accurate).

The *distinctives* discussed here are **not** the fundamentals of the Christian faith. The basic doctrinal position of the assemblies is **not** different from that of the mainstream of orthodox evangelical Christianity. In relation to the *distinctives*, we recognize that there are other orthodox Christians who hold different views and convictions. We respect their views, but we hold on to our convictions to the best of our knowledge and understanding of the Scriptures. It is a part of our rich legacy and stewardship of truth. If these truths are taught in the Word, then they are right. It is not a question of **who** (or which denomination) is right, but **what** is right.

We have to be faithful to the illumination and enlightenment we have received on the truths of God's Word without being judgmental of others who may differ with us. "To his own master he stands or falls" (Rom.14:4). It is very important that we study, know, understand, appreciate, practice and biblically defend these *distinctives* with conviction, courage, grace, humility, and love. We should **not** hold on to them with pride, arrogance, or in a sense of superiority over other Christians.

Rather we must speak the truth in love (Eph.4:15), gentleness and reverence (1 Peter 3:15).

A Word of Caution: The Biblical *distinctives* discussed in this book have nothing to do with "Brethrenism." Sectarianism, denominationalism, legalism, exclusivism, traditionalism, and rigidity are trademarks of "Brethrenism" which erupt from a carnal spirit. It tries to promote and impose man-made rules and traditions as Scriptural doctrines. "Brethrenism" **majors on minors.** Thus the test of orthodoxy is not based on Scripture alone, but also on the "pet" and "peculiar" views held by the advocates of "Brethrenism". In some circles of the Brethren, personal preferences, certain precedents, and traditions are misinterpreted and misrepresented as *distinctives* and imposed on others as doctrines. Anyone who does not subscribe to their ideology is not considered "Brethren." Tightness, rigidity, exclusivism, legalism, and lack of grace are their trademarks. They grossly misrepresent the real Brethren ideals.

This unscriptural trend has adversely affected the initial glory and impact of the Brethren Movement. The biblical principles of the early Brethren began to be legalistically and rigidly interpreted. This served to introduce a definite distortion into the original vision of the Brethren. It is very unfortunate that discord and divisions even over "minor" and "petty" issues have tarnished the testimony of the assemblies in different parts of the world. Biblical separation also have been misinterpreted in some circles as isolation from other Christians. Beware of these dangerous departures! It was W. H. Griffith Thomas who made this remark initially and probably repeated by several others: *"The Brethren rightly divide the Word for others and wrongly divide it among themselves."* How true!

The Brethren historically is a dynamic renewal-revival movement with unswerving commitment to the Word of God. The early Brethren who rediscovered many biblical principles and practiced them enjoyed phenomenal success and growth. Their solid theology was by no means regarded as inimical to their vigorous growth. Even today, the Lord has preserved a testimony for Himself through a faithful remnant that has made a profound impact on Christians all over the world. They have proved that their faith is not a set of dry and dusty theories. Their spiritual dynamism is worthy to be emulated.

This book is **not** an official expression of the faith and practices of the assemblies sanctioned by any group, church, or churches. This is more of a **personal confession of faith** of the author resulting from his fellowship, ministry, and association with the Brethren all through his life, and also based on his personal research and study. There may be assemblies who may no longer hold on to these *distinctives.* Some assemblies may subscribe to most of it, but not all. Still others may support it with some modifications. But the *distinctives* discussed in the following pages generally characterize Christian assemblies in the "open" (distinguished from "exclusive" or similar) Brethren tradition, generally known as "Plymouth Brethren" or "Christian Brethren", or simply "Christians who gather unto the Name of the Lord Jesus Christ" (many of them even do not take the name "Brethren" lest they use it as an unscriptural denominational tag).

A chapter on *Evangelical Distinctives* is also included in the book to put things in perspective. This will also help the readers to appreciate the common biblical heritage the Brethren have with other Christians. We hold the historic Christian faith with all evangelical Christians. That is our common heritage. It is *practice* rather than *doctrine* that distinguishes the Brethren from other conservative evangelical Christians.

What we are concerned here is the rediscovery of the rich biblical legacy of the early Brethren and practice those Scriptural principles in grace and truth. As a result, bold, innovative, and impacting deeds may come out of us that will create powerful and warm-hearted New Testament assemblies. We are committed to the Scriptural truths that were rediscovered in the Brethren Revival Movement. My prayer is that the Lord may help this humble endeavor to be a blessing for the

Brethren to understand themselves better, without misunderstanding everybody else.

"But to this one I will look, to him who is humble and contrite of spirit, and who trembles at My word" *(Isaiah 66:2).*

2

Evangelical Distinctives

"It is a trustworthy statement, deserving full acceptance that Christ Jesus came into the world to save sinners" (1 Tim.1:15)

What is an evangelical Christian? What exactly is evangelical Christianity? What do evangelicals believe? A simple answer is, evangelicals take the Bible seriously as the Word of God and believe in Jesus Christ as Savior and Lord. The term "evangelical" comes from the Greek word *euangelion*, meaning 'the good news" (Gospel). Thus evangelical faith focuses on the good news of salvation through faith in Jesus Christ. **The Savior and the Scriptures** are vitally important in evangelical faith. As commonly used, Evangelical Christianity refers to conservative Protestants. "To be evangelical means to hold to a definite doctrine as well as to participate in a special kind of experience. The experience of the forgiveness of sins through the atoning sacrifice of Christ and the assurance of salvation through the gift of the Spirit will always be paramount in evangelical religion" (Donald G. Bloesch, *Essentials of Evangelical Theology*, Vol.1, Prince Press, 1998, Preface).

Millard J. Erickson, a Baptist theologian, offers a simple and concise definition of evangelicalism: "A movement in modern Christianity emphasizing the gospel of forgiveness and regeneration through personal faith in Jesus Christ, and affirming orthodox doctrines" *(Concise Dictionary of Christian Theology, Baker, 1986, 52)*

Alister McGrath, an evangelical Anglican, offered six major distinctives of Evangelical Christianity:

1. The supreme authority of Scripture
2. Jesus Christ as incarnate God
3. The Holy Spirit
4. Personal conversion
5. Evangelism
6. The importance of the Christian community

(Evangelicalism and the Future of Christianity, IVP, 1995, 55-56)

Historian David Bebbington identifies four qualities as the main evangelical convictions:

1. Biblicism, a particular regard for the Bible.
2. Crucicentrism, a focus on the atoning work of Christ on the cross.
3. Conversionism, the belief that human beings need to be converted.
4. Activism, the belief that the gospel needs to be expressed in effort.

(Evangelicalism in Modern Britain: A History from the 1730s to the 1980s, Unwyn Hyman, 1989, 2-17)

In reality, all true Christians are *evangelical* Christians. Evangelicals have a passion to recapture the vital essence of the Gospel – salvation in Christ. They are committed to the *evangel*, the good news that Jesus Christ is the only Savior of mankind. There is no better news than Jesus!

The Fundamentals of the Faith

Along with all conservative evangelical Christians, the Brethren affirm the fundamentals of the historic Christian faith as outlined below:

1. The full Inspiration (verbal-plenary), inerrancy and infallibility of the Bible.
2. Virgin Birth of our Lord Jesus Christ.
3. The death of Christ on the cross as substitutionary atonement.
4. The bodily resurrection of Christ from the dead.
5. The deity and sinless humanity of Jesus Christ.
6. Salvation by grace through faith alone, and in Christ alone.
7. The literal return of Christ in the Second Advent.

Bible-believing and theologically conservative Christians all over the world hold to these *essentials* as the basic tenets of biblical orthodoxy.

The Central Truths ("The *Solas"*) of the Reformation

The Brethren are deeply committed to the great doctrines of the Reformation:

1. *Sola Scriptura* (Scripture alone)
2. *Sola Fide* (Faith alone)
3. *Sola Gratia* (Grace alone)
4. *Solus Christus* (Christ alone)
5. *Soli Deo Gloria* (To God alone be the glory).

"So far as their doctrines are concerned, Open Brethren have no peculiarities. They hold the historic Christian faith, because they find it plainly taught in the Bible, which is to them, as to all children of the Reformation, 'the only infallible rule of faith and practice.' They are wholeheartedly evangelical in their understanding and presentation of Christianity, proclaiming Jesus Christ, the Son of God, as the all-sufficient Savior of those who put their trust in him and as the only hope for mankind" (F.F. Bruce, "Who Are the Brethren?", Appendix 1, *In Retrospect*, 316).

What we believe does matter. Theology in its practical sense is the art of living unto God. It is the foundation of true spirituality. Any branch of Christianity that is divorced from its theological roots is just a "moral religion" rather than biblical faith that transforms hearts and lives. Theology is a means to an end – a godly life. The function of

24

theology is to preserve the church from fads and novelty. We must reaffirm, define and defend our faith to a new generation. They should know that our faith is **not** built upon the contemporary fads of cultural "churchianity" or on the legalistic traditions of a by-gone era, but on the eternal truths of Biblical Christianity.

"For I delivered to you as of first importance what I also received, that Christ died for our sins according to the Scriptures, and that He was buried, and that He was raised on the third day according to the Scriptures" (1 Cor.15:3-4).

3

A Historical Overview of the Brethren Movement

"Not by might nor by power, but by My Spirit, says the Lord of hosts" (Zech.4:6)

A Revival Movement

Nothing is more thrilling than to read the stories of great revivals. Revival is a special season of spiritual refreshing and renewal when many believers simultaneously experience a deep moving of the Spirit of God in their hearts. One such revival took place in Britain early in the 19th century (around the year 1825) which is commonly known as the "Brethren Movement."

The story of the Brethren Movement is not about the "sleeping" many, but of the "waking" few. Even in the world's deepest "midnight", there have been always children of the "light" and of the "day." In the midst of a slumbering world, they were "awake". God's voice had reached them, His mighty power had raised them, and His holy Word had liberated them.

John Nelson Darby, Edward Cronin, John Gifford Bellet, Francis Hutchinson, William Stokes, Edward Wilson, Anthony Norris Groves, George

Muller and several other young men along with them, were wide "awake" among "sleepers"; the "living" among the "dead." These gifted and well-educated men had deep spiritual convictions. They disregarded all denominational barriers and came together for Christian fellowship, Bible study and to "break bread." Eventually they were separated from all ecclesiastical (denominational) systems and gathered together **"in the name of the Lord Jesus Christ."** The spiritual dynamism of these young "Brethren" significantly altered the image of the 19th century Christendom and made a profound impact on Christian believers all over the world.

It was a time in which many Christians in the British Isles had become dissatisfied by dead orthodoxy and authoritarian clericalism in their denominations. Into this desperate situation came the "Brethren" with their **simpler** and **Scriptural** church principles. They believed that all true believers in Christ belonged to the church (unity of the Body of Christ) and that human ordination was not required by the Scripture to preach the Gospel. They taught that more than one man per church had been gifted by the Holy Spirit for ministry. The new found Scriptural freedom to gather together in the name of the Lord Jesus Christ to "break bread" and remember ("Do this in remembrance of Me") Him without a presiding clergy, was an exciting truth for them. They could not feel at home in the denominational churches to which they originally belonged. Many like-minded Christians found their fellowship and meetings infused by the power of the Holy Spirit and the love of Christ. Their gatherings were marked by New Testament simplicity, passionate devotion to Christ, deep hunger for the Word of God, and sincere love for fellow-Christians.

Beginnings

The little flock of the first "Brethren" (*brethren* is the archaic plural form of *brothers*) gathered in homes and halls for Bible study, prayer, fellowship and breaking of bread (Acts 2:42). Most of these young men were in their mid or late twenties and were associated with Trinity College, Dublin. In **1826,** Edward Cronin and Edward Wilson began meeting together each Lord's Day morning for the breaking of bread, worship, and study of the Word in Edward Wilson's house in Dublin (Wilson was a church deacon and Bible Society secretary at that time). Shortly after this, they moved to Cronin's house and were joined by others (Cronin, who was a medical student and was actively involved in his church, was excommunicated for his views).

There were no ordained leaders, ministers or clergy in their gatherings. Their meetings were open and spontaneous, and spiritual exercises were prompted and guided by the Holy Spirit, though at times one of them also coordinated some of the activities in the services. Other groups with similar convictions started meetings of their own. In November **1829** in Dublin's Fitzwilliam Square, two groups started meeting together in a large room belonging to Hutchinson.

In **1827** when Anthony Norris Groves from England visited Dublin, he suggested to Bellet that they break bread together. This they did in Bellet's home (the weekly "remembrance meeting" "to break bread" became the most cherished distinctive of the Brethren). It was around this time that **John Nelson Darby**, one of the most prominent among the early Brethren, observed the simple kind of communion service for the first time. Many historians identify him as the "founder" of the Brethren movement and the developer of systematic Dispensational Premillennial Theology. He was a man of unusual strength of intellect and personality, who had graduated from Trinity College as classical gold medalist. Although he was selected to the Irish Chancery Bar in 1822, he gave up a career in law to enter church ministry. Darby was ordained as a deacon in 1825 and as a priest in the Church of England in 1826. But he chose to come out of all ecclesiastical ritual and hierarchy, and set apart his life to the ministry of the Gospel, to strengthen the fellowship of the saints who "gathered simply unto the name of the Lord Jesus Christ," and awaited the Lord's imminent return to rapture His own (prophetic themes, especially the hope of the church - the rapture - was a prominent theme among the early Brethren).

J.N. Darby is also known for his Bible translation - **The Darby Bible**, formally known as *The Holy Scriptures: A New Translation from the Original Languages by J.N. Darby*. He also translated the Bible into French and German; quite a brilliant mind! Darby penned his life motto in the lines of this hymn which he composed:

"Oh, the joy of having nothing, and being nothing,
Seeing nothing but a living Christ in glory,
And being careful for nothing,
But his interests down here."

(For a short biography of J. N. Darby, see, Dr. Sunny Ezhumattoor, *A Portrait of John Nelson Darby*, Thekkel Publications, 2006. For a concise history of the Brethren Movement, see *Plymouth Brethren* by the same author).

It is true that the early Brethren founded no Bible Institutes for formal training. But they were outstanding men of learning and many of them were formally trained in disciplines related to the original languages, history, theology and the sciences. They were never against the idea of someone systematically or formally studying the Bible though they always emphasized the Holy Spirit's supreme role in enlightening our minds in the truths of God's Word. These men made use of all the available resources in studying the Word of God. In later generations, some Brethren have opposed the idea of formal biblical education. But this is a very "unbrethren" attitude totally devoid of a sense of history. It is just one example of the ungracious rigidity of some Brethren that recognizes the *form*, but not the *freedom* of the New Testament pattern. Several great men of the Word among the previous generations of the Brethren lacked formal education in biblical and theological studies yet knew the value of such studies and encouraged them for others. They were never opposed to it. They were all diligent students of the Word and studied the Bible thoroughly making use of the available resources at their disposal. Some of them even served as teachers in Bible teaching institutions and also led various training programs for believers.

Plymouth Brethren

Several independent gatherings started all over the British Isles (later spreading to other parts of the world). Revivalism and Scriptural simplicity certainly remained as the major spiritual outlook of these groups. In England, the first Brethren assembly was established in **Plymouth in 1831**. Plymouth was very prominent in the early days of the Brethren Revival. This is the source of the title "Plymouth Brethren." This was not a name taken by them, but rather it was given to them by others. The new group was called by others as the "brothers of Plymouth". Their brotherly love and warmth of fellowship definitely made a deep impression upon all those who observed them. The early Brethren were against all denominational labels. This was part of their core beliefs. They never had the thought of founding a denomination. They referred to themselves as "brethren" or "believers" who "gather unto the name of the Lord Jesus Christ" (and no other name). They preferred that their gatherings be known as "assemblies" than "churches" (to distinguish it from denominational churches).

Two prominent leaders of the Plymouth meeting were **Samuel Prideaux Tregelles** and **Benjamin Wills Newton**. These men were responsible for one of the best *Critical Editions of the Greek New* Testament. Treggelles also wrote a *Hebrew Grammar* and translated Gesenius's *Hebrew Lexicon* from Latin. He was also in the committee overseeing the preparation of the Revised Version.

Bethesda Chapel in Bristol was another important meeting of the Brethren. **George Mueller**, a great hero of faith, who established an orphanage in Bristol (1836), was one of the leading brethren in the Bethesda Chapel. Another leading figure in that meeting was Henry Craik, the son of a

Scottish minister. He was Muller's tutor. It is said that Craik's knowledge of original language was beyond that of most men and his insight into Scripture was unsurpassed.

The first twenty year period of the Brethren Movement can be considered as their "golden era." In the opinion of many historians, at least to some extent, it constituted the most illustrious and edifying chapter in the history of the church since the first century.

Beginning in 1848, a series of divisions divided the Brethren as "**Open**" and "**Exclusive**". It was a split in the Plymouth meeting that led into this fundamental division. It was to those who sided with Darby that the name" "Exclusive Brethren" was given. The Exclusive Brethren have suffered many subsequent splits. Several splinter groups came out of them and were identified usually with the name of a prominent leader among them. They usually have no fellowship with anyone outside of their *exclusive* circle. Exclusive assemblies declined into authoritarianism. What a sad departure from the original ideals of the Brethren!

It is the Open Brethren (this name distinguishes them from the Exclusive Brethren) who are known around the world as *Christian Brethren*, *Independent Brethren* or commonly, as *Plymouth Brethren*. Even among the Open Brethren one will find "tight" or "closed" and even ("open – closed"!) assemblies who may be influenced by some *exclusive* ideas and views (this book is concerned only with matters pertaining to the Open Brethren who strive to follow the biblical distinctives as originally envisioned by the historical Brethren Movement).

The First Brethren Missionary & Overseas Missions

George Muller's brother-in-law, Anthony Norris Groves (1795—1853) is the first overseas missionary of the Brethren. Brethren historians also consider him as the first of the *real* "Open Brethren." He had a pioneering influence that went beyond his personal reach. He gave up his dental practice in Exeter, England, and went to Baghdad, Iraq, as a missionary (1829). He went without the backing of any mission board and no guaranteed means of support; only in total dependence on God. No wonder he is known as the **"Father of Faith Missions."** He was a true disciple who 'took the Cross' and followed his Master. He endured great hardship and personal sacrifice in the mission fields. His wife, Mary Groves, died in a severe epidemic of the plague (1831) and their little girl a few weeks later (*Father of Faith Missions*, an in-depth biography of A. N. Groves by Robert Bernard Dann, Authentic Media, 2004, is highly recommended).

In 1833 Groves came to India and labored for the Lord for almost fifteen years. "Oh!, that a double portion of his spirit would descend on all our drowsy and sleeping churches throughout Christendom" - that was the fervent desire of Alexander Duff, a Presbyterian missionary who had been a colleague of Groves during his missionary work in India. Concerning Groves' ministry and its impact in India, E.H. Broadbent wrote these lines: "......that it would first become possible for true believers to cast aside their denominational differences and exhibit the essential unity of the churches of God in obedience to the Scriptures and in the forbearance of love" (*The Pilgrim Church*, Pickering & Inglis, 1931, 354-55).

Groves exemplified the true spirit of the "Open Brethren" throughout his life. He advocated the New Testament principles of Church and missions wherever he went. He believed that the basis of our fellowship is LIFE in the Christ of Scripture rather than LIGHT on the teachings of the Scriptures. Of course this was the original Brethren ideal. To Groves, our Christian commitment is one of life and love and our fellowship in the life of God through Jesus Christ is a stronger bond than that of being one of us – whether organizationally or denominationally. Sad to say that, many Brethren have departed from this ideal and many are very much opposed to this sentiment. Our preaching, writings, commentaries, actions and attitudes give ample evidence of it every day. This is an area where we need a deep introspection and radical transformation.

The work started by Groves in India witnessed great reviving and enlightening manifestations of the Spirit. Several independent revival movements also fanned the flames of that testimony. The Brethren Movement in India today is more active, growing, and dynamic than in most western countries. India has nearly 3000 assemblies, 2600 full-time evangelists and over 80 assembly institutions.

(For a brief summary on the beginning of the Brethren Movement in India, particularly in Kerala, South India, see *Brethren Distinctives* written in English by Dr. Silas Nair, Brethrenassembly.com/*Ebooks*/Brethren Distinctives; and for more detailed information, see the *History of the World wide Brethren Movement* by T.E. Easaw, written in Malayalam).

One of the most important features of the Brethren Movement is their commitment to global missions. The overseas missions launched by Groves continue in many parts of the world today, leading people to Christ, and establishing New Testament assemblies. It is an unknown fact to many that Jim Elliot, Peter Fleming, and Ed McCully, three of the five young American missionaries who became martyrs in Ecudaor in 1956, were associated with the Brethren. The drive to world missions caused the Brethren to be one of the most aggressive of all the Protestant groups in missions. Church historian

Kenneth Scott Latourette, claims that the Plymouth Brethren missionaries were among the finest in Guatemala, Honduras, Venezuela, India and Indochina around the turn of the last century (*Christianity in a Revolutionary age, Vol.III*, Zondervan, 1970, 312-313,321, 409,424).

Brethren Influence

Though the Brethren assemblies have never been large in number as compared with the great denominations, their influence has been world-wide, and they have made tremendous contributions in the area of theology, Christian literature, and missions. "Brethren" is considered as the single most influential Christian group relative to its size. A wealth of literature, expounding the Scriptures, emanated from this group, and has had far-reaching influence around the world.
"Of all the groups of Christian believers that developed in the English speaking world in the nineteenth century, the one which produced the greatest number of gifted writers was the Brethren" (Wilbur M. Smith).

The dispensational, pretribulational, and premillennial approach to interpreting the Bible was promoted and popularized by the influence of the Brethren Movement (The *Scofield Reference Bible* became known to many as a *handbook of dispensational theology*. This is one of the most influential theological works of the early 20th century). Many denominational and non-denominational Christian congregations have accepted the views of the Brethren on many lines, though they are not openly identified with them.

"For He said, "Surely, they are My people, Sons who will not deal falsely." So He became their Savior" *(Isaiah 63:8).*

Recommended Reading on Brethren History:

Baylis, H. Robert. *My People*. Ontario: Gospel Folio Press, 2006.
Coad, F. Roy. *A History of the Brethren Movement*. Exeter: The Paternoster Press, 1968.
Ironside, H.A. *A Historical Sketch of The Brethren Movement*. Neptune: Loizeaux Brothers, 1985.
Neatby, B. William. *A History of The Plymouth Brethren*. London: Hodder & Stoughton, 1950 (Reprint by FB & C Ltd., 2015).
Pickering, HY. *Chief Men Among The Brethren*. Neptune: Loizeaux Brothers, 1918, 1986.
Rowdon, H. Harold. *The Origins of the Brethren*. London: Pickering & Inglis Ltd., 1967.

4
An Overview of the Distinctives

"But speak thou the things which become sound doctrine" (Titus 2:1, KJV)

The present chapter provides an overview of all the distinctives of the Brethren in summary form (at a glance). However, only the major distinctives will be further developed and explained in the following chapters.

1. **Non-denominational** and non-sectarian. We are *Christians* (*saints, believers, brethren*) who gather unto the name of the Lord Jesus Christ, without attaching significance to any other name or denominational titles. *Brethren* is not used as a denominational label. They have always tried to avoid any distinctive label as they passionately believed in the unity of the Body of Christ.
2. **Christo-centric gathering**. Christ is the gathering center of His people – "gathered unto His name." The *person* and *presence* of Christ is more important than the *place* of gathering.
3. Test of truth is **Scripture alone** (*Sola Scriptura*). The Word of God is the only authority for the Christian faith and practice. Traditions are

subservient to the Scripture, however noble they may be. Traditions and practices that contradict the Bible are not of God and are not a valid aspect of the Christian faith. We are called on to follow the *apostolic traditions* handed down to us through the Word of God, and not any *man-made traditions*.

4. **Priesthood of all believers**. No clergy-laity distinction. Believers in Christ together are a holy and royal priesthood. No humanly ordained ministers, priests, or clergy to do the ministry. All believers are priests and therefore needing no priestly order.

5. Unswerving commitment to the **four pillars of the church** — "apostles' teaching, fellowship, breaking of bread and prayers" (Acts 2:42).

6. **Weekly observance of the Lord's Supper** (breaking of bread) as a part of the corporate worship of the church.

7. **Open and spontaneous worship** with freedom for believers to exercise their spiritual gifts for edification.

8. Emphasis on **fellowship** rather than on church membership.

9. **No one-man pastor**/leader, but a plurality of elders as shepherding leaders in the local assemblies assisted by deacons. Freedom for ministry (service) is open to all believers.

10. **Autonomous and independent** local assemblies as self-governing, and not under any centralized leadership or hierarchical system.

11. Emphasis on **faith ministry**. No salaried ministry or solicitation of funds.
12. **Antioch model of missions** as found in Acts 13. No human ordination, but only commendation to missions and ministry by local assemblies under the guidance of the Holy Spirit.
13. **Silence of women and the veiling of women** (head covering) in the gathering of the church.
14. **Miraculous gifts not seen as normative for today**, and they are not essential to the normal functioning of the church and ministry.
15. **Voluntary Christian giving,** not governed by legalistic rules or tithing.
16. Great emphasis on **discipleship** and **sacrificial living** and a willingness to denounce possessions, pleasures and status of this world.
17. Expectation of the **Lord's imminent return** for His church in the rapture.

"Showing all good faith they may adorn the doctrine of God our Savior" (Titus 2:10).

5

Brethren: Non-Denominational & Non-Sectarian

"…..to the church of God which is at Corinth, to those who have been sanctified in Christ Jesus, saints by calling, with all who in every place call upon the name of our Lord Jesus Christ, their Lord and ours" (1 Cor.1:2)

Denominationalism is man-made, sectarian and divisive. The *Brethren* has never been a denominational name and it was never used as a denominational label by anyone within the movement (at least in its early history). Rather, they were very much opposed to the idea of denominations. Historically, the Brethren Movement was a church renewal movement and not a denominational movement. "Brethren" (brothers) was only a word of greeting for them and never a denominational or official label for their gatherings – they were only "Christians" or "believers" (gathered unto the name of the Lord Jesus Christ). They have always tried to avoid any distinctive label, though names were given to them against their wishes.

F.F. Bruce, a prominent Brethren, made this perceptive observation of the early days of the Brethren movement:

"The founders of the Brethren movement were a group of young men.......who tried to find a way in which they could come together for worship and communion simply as fellow Christians, disregarding denominational barriers. They had no idea that they were starting a movement; still less had they any thought of founding a new denomination, for that would have defeated the very purpose for which they came together" (*In Retrospect*, Appendix 1: Who are the Brethren?" 314.)

In a research article on the *Brethren in North America*, R. H. McLaren made this comment:

"Members of these groups would reject the title. The refusal has a theological base in 1 Corinthians 3:3-6 where the Corinthian church was rebuked for manifesting a party spirit and dividing the body of Christ with each group taking a different name. The name 'Plymouth Brethren' reflects one of the early assemblies, Plymouth, and the common greeting used by its members, "Brethren" (*Emmaus Journal*, Winter/1995, 172).

William MacDonald, who was one of the most respected Bible teachers among the assemblies in America, has addressed the issue of a denominational name:

"We must never forget that we are Christians, believers, brethren, disciples and saints – and so are all who have been redeemed by the precious blood of Christ. To deny this by any form of sectarianism, denominationalism or exclusivism is to deny the truth of the Bible and to be guilty of carnality and pride" (*To What Should We Be Loyal?* Walterick Publishers, 10).

H. A. Ironside, who was connected with the Brethren for over forty years has traced their history in his book *A Historical Sketch of the Brethren Movement* (Loizeaux Brothers, 1985). This is what he wrote in this book about the name "Brethren".

".......for those who hold the principles of gathering which I purpose examining in these papers, have from the first refused any names that would be distinctive or that could not be applied rightfully to all of God's people. Therefore, they speak of themselves as brethren, believers, Christians, saints, or use any other term that is common to all members of the body of Christ. With this explanation, I trust I shall give offense to none in speaking of them hereafter as the Brethren, and using the capital in order to make clear who are intended, though its use is utterly condemned by these Christians themselves" (9-10).

The non-denominational character of the assemblies is also explained by H.G. Mackay in his popular book *Assembly Distinctives*.

"One of the outstanding features of a denomination is a distinguishing name and when such a name is retained, even in an independent position, that church cannot be said to be undenominational. But the assemblies reject all divisive names, even though such are given to them against their wishes. It has already been pointed out that all distinguishing names are rejected by the great majority of Christians in fellowship in local assemblies. "Brethren," "Plymouth Brethren," "Exclusive Brethren," "Open Brethren," etc. are all names applied to the assemblies, but are not accepted by them" (*Assembly Distinctives*, Everyday Publications, 1981,30).

The great poet, Mahakavi K. V. Simon, who was one of the outstanding leaders of Kerala's (South India) evangelical reformation movement, a champion of biblical orthodoxy, and also a pioneer among the Indian Brethren, clearly understood the non-denominational and non-sectarian character of the Brethren movement. He wrote about this in the *History of the Assemblies in Kerala* (in Malayalam language). In his introduction he states that the brethren are known by various names including, Baptist, Brethren, Non-denominational Church etc. and there is no strict label for them. Different names should not deter us from accepting one another (see page ii).

K.V. Simon also points to the fact that many of the biblical doctrines that are held very dearly by the assemblies came to light in Kerala through the preaching and Bible classes of the Baptist missionary Gregson (see pages 79-81). To affirm the unity of the Church, which is a primary doctrine of the Brethren, K.V. Simon has included Gregson's tract entitled "Members of One Body" in his book (74-77). This tract, completely endorsed by K. V. Simon, strongly argues for his understanding of the non-denominational character of the assemblies (It is deplorable that some Kerala Brethren depict K.V. Simon as a strong Brethren denominationalist who was totally intolerant of all other Christian believers who did not have the "Brethren" label!).

In the *History of the World-wide Brethren Movement*, written in Malayalm by an Indian author, evangelist T.E. Easow, the strong non-denominational character of the movement is emphasized (46-47; 70-73; 77-79). Justus Samuel, who was a prominent leader among the assemblies in India, in his book *The Brethren*, has clearly shown the unscripturalness of taking the appellation 'Brethren' to indicate a denomination. He recalls the principles of the early Brethren who had absolutely no intention of launching a new denomination. "Christians, who happened to have the appellation 'Brethren' attached to themselves, actually were against a denominational tag thus being fixed on them" (17, see also 9-19). It seems that many Indian brethren have forgotten all about these matters!

A Warning

Beware! Some Brethren who claim all these truths about the non-denominational character of the Brethren can be very denominational and sectarian in their attitude and practice. You will get a feel for it the moment you walk into their assemblies. There are heart-breaking stories to that effect from assemblies around the world. This writer himself has witnessed such unchristian and unscriptural attitudes exhibited to fellow-believers and barring them basic Christian fellowship in assemblies just because they do not carry a "Brethren" label, or they do not conform to a particular "brand" of *Brethren*! What an unchristian attitude! It still continues in many assemblies. No wonder the lampstands have been removed from places that were once the stronghold of the Brethren.

Since the Brethren strongly emphasized the Scriptural teaching of the **unity of the Body of Christ**, they opposed all sectarian thinking that would violate this precious truth. Wherever there is *Brethren denominationalism*, it disregards these precious truths. This is "Brethrenism" and does not represent the true spirit and teaching of the Brethren.

Sectarianism is Unscriptural

There is a Scriptural reason the Brethren did not favor a name or a label. Exclusive, party line, and sectarian thinking is condemned in the Bible. "I am of Paul," and "I of Apollos," and "I of Cephas", and "I of Christ." Has Christ been divided?" (1 Cor.1:12-13). Again Paul writes: "......for you are still fleshly......For when one says, "I am of Paul", and another, "I am of Apollos", are you not mere men?" (1 Cor.3:3-4). Sects or parties were formed within the Corinthian church. There were four parties, though the servants of God were not responsible for it. The presence of such divisions in Corinth was a sign of carnality, and a denial of the unity of the body of Christ (the church) which is a fundamental truth in the New Testament. No wonder, we find Paul's indignant rebuke of sectarianism.

The term "church" is never used in the Bible for a denomination. The denominational sense is foreign to the Word of God. That sense suggests there is a division in the body of Christ and that is why the Bible never uses the word in a denominational sense. In all the teachings of the Brethren on church truths, the unity of the body of Christ was emphatic - the church is the body of Christ made up of all true believers (1 Cor.12:27).

"One of the most obvious truths is the unity of the body of Christ. There is only one body, one church, one assembly (Eph.4:4). Because this is true, all believers are responsible to bear witness to it. As we gather together, we should give practical expression to it. Nothing that we do or say should deny it" (William MacDonald, *To What Should We Be Loyal?* 9). But the sad fact is that this is constantly denied in many assemblies though theoretically they claim to be non-denominational and non-sectarian.

Some Practical Suggestions

Remember that we are "Christians", "believers", "saints" who have been redeemed by the blood of the Lamb. We do not belong to any sect or denomination. We belong to the Lord and to Him alone. We gather in His name and are committed to obey His Word. We refuse to take any name that will fragment the Church of Jesus Christ.

Let us recognize that there are many true Christians around us who love the Lord and follow Him. **Let us not think exclusively of us as the Lord's people**. In a given geographical area, we are a gathering of God's people that meets at a particular location. Our gathering and fellowship in a local church is based upon Scriptural truths about which we are convinced of. Let us be faithful to our convictions and honorably maintain the **stewardship of truth** that is committed to us. We don't have to make any unscriptural compromise. With anyone. We are called on to judge everything by the Word of God alone. "To his own master he stands or falls...Let each man be fully convinced in his own mind" (Rom.14:4-5).

How will we answer the question, **"What denomination are you?"** We are Christians. Jesus Christ is our Savior and Lord. We are non-denominational, independent Christian assemblies seeking to practice the principles of the New Testament. We are generally known by the name given to us by others, "Brethren." Believing that the Church is one body, composed of all believers, we refuse to take any name that is not common to all Christians. We meet weekly to practice Acts 2:42: "And they were continually devoting themselves to the apostles' teaching and to fellowship, to the breaking of bread and to prayer."

Can We Ever Use the Name "Brethren"?

This is not an easy question to answer. But the question needs to be addressed. We are living amidst the denominational confusion in Christendom. In some countries today, especially where Christians are a minority and often persecuted, the government of the land has mandated rules that all churches, church organizations, funds, mission and service agencies etc. must be registered with the government with respective denominational names. This is an absolute necessity now in many places if Christians have to get their rights, protection, representation, tax filings and exemptions, and even for carrying out regular activities. **A label or an identifying name becomes a necessity in such situations.** This is an undeniable fact.

Believers in many Western countries with full religious freedom may not really understand the challenges our fellow-believers face in other lands. Practical solutions are needed to face these challenges. In certain mission fields, where the pioneers ignored these challenges and did not help the churches, many assemblies lost their New Testament identity. Believers did not know what to do due to divided opinions, lack of teaching, counsel, and mature leadership. Many leaders approached such situations with poor judgment and ungracious rigidity. Eventually this caused divisions and some assemblies joined with liberals, Charismatics and other denominations, not holding on to sound doctrine. Others opted to register with a name. This writer happened to visit a country to help in the assembly missions, where a denominational "bishop" is leading the first Brethren assembly there, founded by very conservative Brethren missionaries!

What shall we do in such situations? We have a responsibility to be *realistic* about these issues and help our fellow-believers with *prudent and practical* counsel with *pastoral* concern. In the confusion created by the denominations today, there are situations when we have to identify our brand of Christianity. A doctrinal statement of our faith with non-denominational emphasis may not be much of a help in this regard, especially when we deal with non-Christians and pagans who have no idea about what we are talking about. In certain countries, having no name may be interpreted even as a cult.

When we have to identify ourselves with a name, or where it is a *help* rather than a *hindrance* in Christian testimony, there is nothing essentially wrong in using an appropriate name, **not as a denominational title, but only as an identifying name**. The Lord knows such situations. In this sense for the purpose of *identification and communication* (not in a denominational or sectarian sense), to avoid confusion and hindrance to our testimony and ministry, if one has to use a name, I do not think we have to make a big issue out of it. We have to be realistic, practical, relevant, gracious and understanding in our approach in such matters. The assemblies need more godly elders with practical wisdom to lead the people of God in such situations.

Some Christians also may wish to use a name on a **confessional level** (I am personally inclined to it) to let others know that they share a set of theological convictions shared by assemblies of Christians generally known under a particular name. On a proper confessional level, I believe, a name can also stimulate mature, reflective theological thinking. One may use the name "Brethren" to identify themselves with Christians of certain doctrinal convictions, who uphold the great biblical truths that were rediscovered in the historical revival movement generally referred to as the Brethren Movement.

There is no escape from the denominational confusion and mess in the world. However we eschew denominationalism, it sticks to us. Our responsibility is to know that **we are Christians and not denominationalists**. Non-denominational and independent churches, Brethren, Bible Churches, House Churches, Local Church Movement etc., are considered by others as denominations, though they are not typical denominations. *It is ironic that denying denominationalism, several Christian groups have succeeded in creating more denominations and trying to run from denominationalism, they only increased it.* Even many assemblies, who deny denominationalism and a name, tend to be more denominational and sectarian in all their practices.

We believe it is always better to go by the simple title "Christian." Denominationalism was not at all a problem during New Testament times, though the spirit of sectarianism was present in its incipient form (in the Corinthian assembly). But the present day Christian faces an entirely different situation. A new believer can be totally confused by a host of denominations, each claiming to follow the Bible. In the midst of this confusion, there may be situations when an **identifying name** is necessary.

We should not forget that there is a marked difference between the simplicity of the New Testament days, and the complexity of these days.

One must remember that even the very name "Christian" was not a name given to us by Christ. Believers were first called "Christians" ("Christ's people" or "Christ-ones") by the people of Antioch (Acts 11:26) as a nick name, maybe even in a derogatory sense. Even in our "holy" and "pious" claims, there can be pride and carnality. Those Christians in Corinth who claimed that they *only* followed Christ are still condemned by Paul as he includes the label "of Christ" (1 Cor.1:11-13).

The issue of a name is not at all a major doctrinal issue. Then why did we discuss it here at length? The presentation here may be vulnerable to misunderstanding or misinterpretation. But this writer chose to take that risk for a greater good. Many believers in different parts of the world need a balanced counsel as they are confronted by many practical problems (my missions and ministry experience for the last 40 years have prompted me to be more helpful, practical, and realistic). Just a theological lecture will not help them. I have received numerous questions with reference to these matters. None of the reasons presented here constitute a *requirement* or an *argument* to use a name. But I believe it is *permissible* for the right reason, at the right time, with a right motive, for those who choose to do so.

A denominational or sectarian thought never occurred to me while writing this book on the "Brethren" and using that name. It is used as a **descriptive term** or a **term of identification**. It is a **convenient designation** which can have a confessional flavor also. This should not be misunderstood. It is safe to say that we do not use it as a sectarian or denominational name, but may use it as a descriptive or identifying name. Expressions such as "the meetings of the Brethren", "Brethren conference", "the writings of the Brethren, "the Brethren movement, "origins of the Brethren", "Chief men among the Brethren" etc. are in common use today and no one considers it as heretical.

We must also remember that any gathering of believers that share a set of values, or doctrinal commitments (or distinctives), even if they call themselves non-denominational, independent, a movement, a fellowship, is functionally identified as a denomination (as far as the English language is concerned) by others.

Many of us are like John Bunyan, the author of *Pilgrims Progress* who was against all denominational names. He believed that these names came from "hell and Babylon." It seems finally he realized one could not ultimately escape from all labels. In his book *The Heavenly Footman*, Bunyan exhorts his readers: "….and be sure thou have a care of Quakers, Ranters, Freewillers; also do

55

Faith and Practices of the Brethren

not have too much company with Anabaptists, though I go under that name myself" (Project Gutenberg E Book, www.gutenberg.org/files/13750).

"Church" or "Assembly"?

The usage of the term *assembly* is not considered a major distinctive of the Brethren, though Brethren usually refer to their gatherings as *assemblies*. But many believers today ask questions about the validity of using the term *church* instead of *assembly*. In the past, some Brethren writers have portrayed the use of *assembly* as a distinctive and have made a doctrine of unjustifiable proportion out of it.

The Brethren usually refer to their meetings as *assemblies* than *churches*. The Greek word *ekklesia* refers to the "assembly" or "congregation", "a called-out company". Hence **"assembly" is the most accurate translation of** *ekklesia*. The emphasis of this word is on the fact of a gathering. The first English Bible translated from Greek (William Tyndale's translation in 1526) correctly translated *ekklesia* as "congregation." But in the authorized version of 1611, King James insisted that the ecclesiastical word "church" should be used (some of us need to be reminded that KJV is not of Brethren origin!).

The English term *church* is derived from the Greek *kuriakon*, and means, "belonging to the

56

Lord." Its application to the church stems from its use by the early Christians for the place where they met together (denoting the idea that it belongs to the Lord). Since the word *church* is associated with buildings of worship, and also because of its denominational usage in Christendom, the Brethren always preferred the term *assembly* as it reflects the **true meaning of the word *ekklesia***. We have **no** quarrel with the word *church*, but prefer to use *assembly* by choice.

The buildings associated with the Open Brethren are usually called "Bible Chapel", "Gospel Chapel", "Gospel Hall, "Christian Assembly," etc. (some Gospel Halls tend to be more *tight, rigid,* or *closed* in certain practices than most "open" assemblies). *Church* in modern English is a widely used term to denote a local Christian congregation or assembly, as well as buildings of Christian worship and denominations. It practically communicates the fact that it is in reference to the gathering of Christians. Hence, there is nothing wrong in using the term *church* (in some countries it is a necessity and is more helpful to evangelism and missions). It must be remembered that church in the biblical sense is the assembly of people called out by God. In the Bible it is **never** used to denote a building, or in a denominational or sectarian sense.

Anywhere in the world today, *church* conveys the idea of a Christian gathering more than *assembly, chapel,* or *hall.* Some of these terms may make sense among the English speaking people, but not in other parts of the world. Even in Western countries these terms are sometimes misunderstood. Some may not like the term 'church' because it is so misused today. That is true. But just because a term is misused does not mean we cannot use it in the proper scriptural sense. For example, Mormons call their leaders 'elders' but that does not mean we should stop using the term 'elder' in the right way. 'Praise and worship' are misused terms in many churches today, but that does not mean we should stay away from those terms altogether.

Let us be careful not to blow things out of proportion. In matters pertaining to our faith, we have to be practical and relevant without contradicting biblical truths. Otherwise, we become irrelevant in our ministry to our generation. In many assemblies, believers are confused in simple matters that were highlighted in this chapter. People argue and quarrel over such things. The main reason is the lack of able leadership with balanced and mature understanding of the Word who can teach and counsel the people of God.

"Being diligent to preserve the unity of the Spirit in the bond of peace" (Eph.4:3).

6

"Gathered Unto His Name"

"God first concerned Himself about taking from among the Gentiles a people for His name"
(Acts 15:14)

We believe in **Christo-centric** gathering – gathered unto the name of the Lord Jesus Christ alone; no other names other than the name of the Lord Jesus Christ. He is the gathering center of His people. "....where two or three have gathered together in My name, there I am in their midst" (Matt.18:20). The *person* of Christ is more important than the *place* of gathering. It is the name of Christ (and no other name) that draws His people together. He is the exclusive focus of gathering.

Christ's name expresses His authority, character, glory, majesty, and all that He is. Christ is the magnet that draws His people together. We are drawn together by what we have found in Him, our Savior and Lord. To gather in His name is to recognize His supremacy, preeminence, authority, to be occupied with Himself, in acknowledgement of all that He is, to seek His glory, in obedience to His Word. What a glorious truth!

In the book of Revelation, the Lord was seen by John in the midst of the seven golden lampstands (Rev.1:13). These lampstands represent the seven churches of Asia (Rev.1:20). The Lord is in the center of the churches. He has the central place among His people. They are around Him alone, under His sole authority. He is the risen head of His church.

In 1 Samuel 22:2, we read about four hundred men who "gathered" to David. It says of David in regard to them that "he became captain over them." The people who gather to the Lord should be willing to accept His authority in all areas of life – the Lordship of Christ. How can we claim the promise in Matt.18:20, if we are divisive and quarrel with one another?

C.H. Mackintosh expressed the importance of the Scriptural truth of gathering unto His name in these powerful words:

"It is around the person of a living Christ, then, that God's assembly is gathered. It is not around a doctrine, however true; nor around an ordinance, however important; but around a living, divine Person. This is a great cardinal and vital point which must be distinctly seized, tenaciously held, and faithfully and constantly avowed and carried out" ("The All-Sufficiency of the Name of Jesus" in *The Mackintosh Treasury*, Loizeaux Brothers, 1976, 819).

The name of the Lord Jesus Christ is above every other name. The Father has highly exalted the Son and bestowed on Him the name which is above every name (Phil.2:9). Repentance and remission of sins is to be preached in His name (Luke 24:47). There is no other name under heaven that has been given among men, by which we are saved (Acts 4:12). The church is to pray in His name (John16:23-24) and to enforce discipline in His name (1 Cor.5:4); gather in His name (Matt.18:20), and do everything in His name (Col.3:17). "God is not unjust so as to forget your work and the love which you have shown toward His name" (Heb.6:10). "Let everyone who names the name of the Lord abstain from wickedness" (2Tim.2:19). There is no sweeter name than the blessed name of our Savior! As the hymn writer expressed it:

"A sweeter sound than Thy blest name; O Savior of mankind!"

As we claim this distinctive, let us listen to a very timely advice given by William MacDonald: "No group can claim to be the only ones who meet in His name; if that were so, His presence would be limited to a small segment of His body on earth. Wherever **two or three are gathered** in recognition of Him as Lord and Savior, he is **there in the midst**" (*Believer's Bible Commentary*, Thomas Nelson, 1995, 1274).

"The name of the LORD is a strong tower; the righteous runs into it and is safe" (Prov.18:10).

61

7

Autonomous and Independent

"The One who holds the seven stars in His right hand, the one who walks among the seven golden lampstands" (Rev.2:1)

The New Testament is the only sufficient and authoritative constitution of the church. An understanding of New Testament ecclesiology (the doctrine of the church) will disclose the autonomous and independent nature of the local church. *To be 'autonomous' is to be self-governing. To be 'independent' is to be free from any outside control or religious hierarchy. We are independent of denominational ties and affiliation.* The Bible does not support the concept of an ecclesiastical hierarchy, "center" or headquarter to govern and determine the ministry, functions and decisions of the local congregations. The Brethren assemblies follow this Scriptural pattern.

The churches established by the apostles of the Lord Jesus Christ were all autonomous and independent. They were free from any outside control by a synod, conference, presbytery, association, or central organization. Each local church was viewed as a self-governing body directly responsible to the Lord. A local assembly is solely governed by the elders (whom God has raised up from within the assembly), and is in no way subject to outside leadership or legislation. The New Testament record clearly affirms the autonomy of the local assembly. We do not believe in a centrally administered system of church government. "The absence of the New Testament record of any church officials with jurisdictional authority extending beyond the local assembly militates against the notion of an organizational union of churches" (H.G. Mackay, *Assembly Distinctives*, 28).

The New Testament Pattern

1. Each local church chose its own officers (Acts 6:1-6).
2. Each exercised its own discipline (1 Cor.5:13)
3. Internal problems were handled by the congregation (1 Cor.6:1- 8).
4. The maintenance of sound doctrine was the responsibility of the local assembly (1 Tim.3:15; Rev.2:14-16).
5. The Holy Spirit directs each local group of believers (Acts 13:1-3).
6. Each local church was not responsible to any higher ecclesiastical body, but was subject and accountable only to Him who is the Head of the church (Rev.2-3).
7. An aggregation of local churches was never looked upon organizationally as a "church," but

always as "churches" (plural) referring to a number of churches in a given geographical area, emphasizing the individual prerogatives of each congregation (Rom.16:16; 1 Cor.16:1; 16:19; 2 Cor.8:1).

8. There is organization *within* a local church (elders, deacons), but this is not an organization *of* churches (Phil.1:1; Acts 6:1-6). There was no outward form of organization between New Testament churches, and no centrally administered church government.

The Lord and the Churches (Rev.1-3)

The seven churches of Asia in the first three chapters of the Book of Revelation are likened to seven golden lampstands (1:11, 12, and 19). The light of life and testimony shone from each lampstand. There was no *Asian Church* of which each of the seven assemblies was a constituent part, as we find in most of Christendom today.

The Lord Jesus walked in the midst of these churches. He is actively present among His people. Each church was individually addressed, commended, corrected, and counselled. The churches themselves do not rebuke or correct one another. None was held accountable for the actions of others. The Lord did not ask or authorize one church to take disciplinary action against another church. Each local church is directly under the authority of the Lord and they are accountable to Him who is the head of the church. "The seven are all mutually independent as to external order and government, yet they are meant to be one in the unity of the Spirit, under the one headship of Christ" (J. M. Davies, *The Lord* And *The Churches*, Walterick Publishers, 1967, 116).

There is no higher court of appeal in the New Testament than the local assembly (Matt.18:15-20). Church discipline is to be carried out only by the local assembly. The assembly *may* seek, if necessary, the guidance and counsel of mature believers from other assemblies in dealing with difficult issues, situations, or problems. There is no authorized general body of believers or assemblies (or assembly representatives) who have the authority to carry out disciplinary action against a believer. "In Israel, troubles which could not be settled locally were to be taken to the place where the Lord had established His name (Deut.17:8-13). But today there is no geographical center established as a clearing house for the disposal of assembly difficulties" (J.M. Davies, *The Lord And The Churches*, 26).

The Jerusalem Council & the
Autonomy of the Local Church

The council of Jerusalem (Acts 15) does not contradict the principle of autonomy of the local church. The immediate occasion of the Jerusalem council was the visit to Syrian Antioch of some Jewish Christians from Jerusalem, and their teaching that circumcision was essential to salvation. A team from the church at Antioch, consisting of Paul and Barnabas and certain others, were sent to Jerusalem to meet with the "apostles and elders" concerning this matter. So the so-called "Jerusalem Council" was basically a conference held between delegates from the Church of Antioch with the apostles and elders at Jerusalem.

After discussing the matter and recognizing the vital importance of the issues involved, the Jerusalem church ("the apostles and elders with the whole church, Acts 15:22) sent two of its leading men with a letter to Antioch, clarifying the issues and undermining the wrong teachings of the Judaizers (Acts 15:22-29).

Ryrie's summary of the circumstances leading to the Jerusalem council is very helpful:

"The problems raised by the presence of the Gentiles in the Church came to a head. Peter had learned that no man should be called unclean – not even Gentiles (10:34), and the Jerusalem church had accepted the first Gentile converts on an equal basis with Jewish converts and without the necessity of being circumcised. However, the ultra-Judaistic party went on the offensive and insisted that Gentiles converts be circumcised. A parallel question was also being raised. Should there be unrestricted social contacts between Jewish and Gentile Christians? The Judaistic party separated themselves from those who did not follow the dietary laws and would not partake of the common meals. Chapter 15 is concerned with these two questions: circumcision and foods (socializing). Had the division over these questions prevailed the unity of the church would have been shattered from the start" (*The Ryrie Study Bible*, New American Standard Translation, Moody Press, 1978, 1673).

Some salient features of the Jerusalem council are noted below:

1. The decision of the Antioch church to go to Jerusalem was purely **voluntary**. The Jerusalem church had no organizational authority or superiority which demanded their coming.
2. It was a special gathering (a consultation) for a special purpose. The apostles and elders were not meeting in permanent session, with Jerusalem headquarters, to discuss various problems in the assemblies and impose their verdict on all the local assemblies. The terms in

67

which the elders wrote the letter is **devoid of any authoritarian or imposing language** (according to F.F. Bruce, "no strong verbs of commanding"). It was not a binding edict.

3. The decision of the apostles and elders were totally under the **guidance of the Holy Spirit** – "It seemed good to the Holy Spirit and to us" (Acts 15:28). Since they humbly sought the mind of the Holy Spirit in this matter, fellowship between Jewish and Gentile believers were strengthened. That the Jerusalem church addressed the Gentiles as "brethren" was significant (Acts 15:23).

William MacDonald offers this helpful observation about the Jerusalem council:

"........this was not an official body with regulatory powers. It was simply a gathering of apostles and elders acting in an advisory capacity. The council did not summon the men to come from Antioch; the latter decided to consult the men in Jerusalem. The decision of the council was not binding on the churches; it was simply offered as the combined judgment of the group" (*Believer's Bible Commentary*, 1632).

Independent Yet Interdependent

Though local churches are autonomous and *independent,* they are *interdependent* for mutual fellowship, evangelization and other united ministries for the glory of God and the blessing of His people. They may seek help or counsel from neighboring assemblies, or invite visiting teachers from other assemblies. Some assemblies are barely surviving as their numbers have considerably declined. It will be a wise step to merge with another assembly in the locality or they may seriously consider how to revive the existing group. Anemic, weak, inactive and bare survival does not seem to be a pattern in the New Testament.

Decisions or actions of one assembly *may* (or *may not*) affect or influence another assembly. They are not under obligation to any other assembly or group of assemblies. No one can impose or force them to accept a decision by another assembly. Each assembly is totally cast upon the Lord for guidance and decisions. They must exercise their spiritual discernment in this matter.

A healthy and balanced perspective is needed in the matter of *independence* and *interdependence.* These two truths must be maintained properly to give visible and tangible proof of Christian unity, love, and service. Failure to act in cooperation and unity with fellow-believers, the church ceases to give one of the most effective possible forms of testimony to the world.

Commenting on the autonomous spirit, Deffinbaugh wrote these penetrating words:

"We dare not be independent of all others in our interpretation of Scripture, in a way that suggest that only we have found the truth and proclaim it. We dare not be independent of other churches in our sense of obligation to them. The distinguishing mark of Christians and of churches is their unity, not their independence. Thus, the church at Antioch expressed its unity with the church in Jerusalem in several ways. It accepted Barnabas when he was sent to them (Acts 11:22-24). It sent money to the "brethren in Judea" when word of the famine was prophesied (Acts 11:27-30). It also appealed to the church leaders in Jerusalem when the gospel was challenged by the Judaizers (Acts 15:1-3). The autonomy of the local church is a doctrine which needs to be very carefully defined and practiced. It should hardly be the watchword. Unity is the distinguishing mark of the church which Paul consistently stressed (Eph.4)" [Robert L. Deffinbaugh, *"The Characteristics of a Cult"* (Acts 15:1-31), www.bible.org].

Organizationally, the churches in the New Testament were clearly independent, but *organically* they were directly and inseparably joined to the Head of the Church, the Lord Jesus Christ. This truth is a profound reminder for local assemblies to respect the *independence* and *interdependence* they share with others. As such, each church has the opportunity and obligation to partner in various levels of Christian life and ministry such as shared resources, shared suffering, shared encouragement, shared ministries, shared accountability, shared orthodoxy etc.

No church government is biblical which fails to recognize and practically demonstrate the unity of the church. Harping on the doctrine of independence, at the expense of unity will betray our testimony in the world. Some Brethren have stretched the doctrine of the autonomous and independent nature of the assemblies to *extreme* and unhealthy positions and have *overlooked* the **importance of interdependence**. They have made independence the watchword to their own peril. They do not cooperate with other assemblies, and do not encourage, take part or support any united efforts by the people of God. Even when they are barely surviving as an assembly, they do not seek or welcome the help of ministering brothers from other assemblies or open avenues for help, fellowship and cooperation. Sometimes this is due to very rigid policies or the unwillingness to accept other brethren who may have different views on non-essential matters. Some assemblies only cooperate with their particular *brand* of Brethren.

71

They remain so *isolated* from others to their own demise (too independent and individualistic ecclesiology!). Eventually, they close down; the lampstand is removed. What a sad story!

How can assemblies show/practice interdependence? That will be for the assemblies in each area to consider, plan and implement. A 'one size fits all' approach will not work. United efforts in evangelistic outreach, conducting special studies/seminars together, having a united book room/library, sharing of resources, planning short term missions trips etc. are just examples of things that can be done.

"On the one hand anything savoring of affiliation must be avoided, and on the other, local church autonomy should not militate against united activities for specified purposes. We must not be like the people of Laish who had 'no business with any man.' They were easily overcome (Judges 18:27, 28) [J. M. Davies, *The Lord And The Churches*, 26-27]. Let us heed to this wise counsel!

"Behold, how good and how pleasant it is for brothers to dwell together in unity" (Psalm133:1).

8

The Priesthood of Believers

"You also, as living stones, are being built up as a spiritual house for a holy priesthood" (1 Peter 2:5)

The Brethren assemblies have a splendid history as champions of the doctrine of the *Priesthood of Believers*, though there are other Christian groups who subscribe to this truth. This doctrine means that all believers in Jesus Christ are priests unto God, and hence they have the privilege of direct access unto God, without any human mediator or ecclesiastical institution.

There is no "clergy" and "laity" distinction in the Bible. This unscriptural distinction is deeply entrenched in Christendom today. In some denominations it is rigidly practiced, and in others, in a lesser and subtle way. This artificial distinction is solely based upon ecclesiastical traditions. One has to distinguish between the *priesthood of Christendom* and *true Christian priesthood*. The idea of a 'priestly class' which exercises functions forbidden to other believers is nowhere found in the New Testament. Though the *Priesthood of Believers* was a cardinal truth of the Reformation, due to clericalism, it has eclipsed in several denominations that claim Reformation tradition.

The Church as Priesthood

The church is a "holy temple in the Lord" (Eph.2:21), and a temple is not complete without a priesthood to minister in it. Believers are a community of priests (1 Pet. 2:5, 9; Rev.1:6; 5:10; 20:6). We have perfect liberty and access through Him to enter into the very Holy of Holies for communion, prayer, and worship (Heb.10:19-22). The nature of the church is a "spiritual house" and its vocation is a holy priesthood. We have been called and chosen to minister in the sanctuary of God. It is a marvelous privilege and opportunity to be a priestly people serving the King of Kings and Lord of Lords.

Israel was called a kingdom of priests (Exo.19:5-6).They enjoyed the privileges of it while neglecting its responsibility. Thus, they forfeited their national ministry. A special priesthood was chosen by God to represent even the nation before God. *Israel had a priesthood, but the church is a priesthood.* By the death of Christ the old order of priesthood was finished and a new order of priesthood was introduced. On the basis of the finished work of Christ, every believer has free access into the very presence of God. Now the theme of a priestly nation is directly applied to the church (1 Peter 2:9).

We **collectively** are a spiritual priesthood. The "priesthood" concept emphasizes our "access" into the presence of God, and the corporate role the church in worship, witness, intercession, anᵤ ministry. As **"holy priesthood"** we minister to God by offering up spiritual sacrifices (1Peter 2:5). As **"royal priesthood"** we proclaim the praises of Him who has called us out of darkness into His marvelous light (1 Peter 2:9). As royal priests, we serve the King of Kings and we will reign with Him one day and minister in His Kingdom (Rev.1:6; 5: 10; 20:6).

In 1 Peter chapter 2, Peter is referring to our collective ministry and responsibility. The exercise of holy priesthood is *vertical – offering up*; the exercise of royal priesthood is *horizontal – declaring*. One is directed to God and the other to man. One involves worship, the other testimony. As holy priests we minister to the heart of God, whereas as royal priests we minister to the house of God. As holy priests we go into the sanctuary, as royal priests we go outside the camp (bearing His reproach as we witness to the world). As priests we worship God and minister to people in service and witness. What a glorious calling and responsibility!

Sacrifices of the Priesthood

At least four sacrifices of the priesthood are suggested in the New Testament as the functions of the priesthood:

1. Our own bodies (Rom.12:1).
2. Our praise (Heb.13:15).
3. Our good deeds and financial stewardship (Heb.13:16).
4. Our ministry (Rom.15:16).

This is similar to the functions of the Old Testament priesthood – the service of the **altar** (sacrifices), the service of **witness** (proclamation of the Law), and the service of **intercession** for the people.

Practice of the Priesthood of Believers in Church Life

In our worship and ministry, in the assemblies, we really enjoy the blessings of the doctrine of the priesthood of believers as we endeavor to faithfully apply it in all aspects of our church life. The "open" time of worship (worship is the work of a priest), and the freedom in ministry, and the liberty to exercise one's spiritual gifts are a splendid demonstration of the truth of this vital doctrine. There are no humanly ordained priests or ministers in the assembly who dominate or control the ministries of the church. We acknowledge Jesus

Christ as the Great High Priest of His people and the only Head of the Church, and the believers together are the holy priesthood. The idea of the priesthood of believers is one of the most precious and powerful images of Scripture.

What does it mean to be a priest? This is a question each one of us has to ponder over **Scripturally** and **practically**. In my estimation, the doctrine of the priesthood of believers, in which we often claim *superiority* over others, is misused and even abused in several assemblies, either by ignorance or selfishness. Many believers understand it only in terms of its **privileges** without any regard to its **responsibilities**. Does this doctrine mean each one of us can interpret Scripture in any way we like, without any regard to hermeneutical principles? Does this mean that one can obstinately push his/her rights and opinions with little regard to the needs of others or the interest of the assembly? Does this doctrine give us a license to totally disregard the recognition and unique role of **equipping leaders** in the church (Eph.4:11-12)? Have we wrongly interpreted the doctrine of the priesthood of believers as the **"Preacherhood of all Believers"**?

Many believers in our assemblies have the false notion that since we believe in the priesthood of believers, we all can or should *preach* and *teach*. Sometimes we proudly say, "We don't have a "one-man" pastor, but that "anybody" can speak in our meeting." We fail to make the distinction between priesthood and the ministry of the Word which is to be done **only by gifted men** in the assembly for the edification of all. The gifted men of the Word also should be empowered by the Holy Spirit. There should be *power* for the fruitful exercise of the gifts.

It seems that in many assemblies, we have opened our pulpit too wide to accommodate *any* and *every one* without due consideration of their utterance gifts; all in the name of the doctrine of the priesthood of believers! When we do this we are doing a disservice to the people of God. It is high time that we "fence" our pulpit. This is an area where our elders have to be more discerning and responsible. The primary duty of teaching the word is vested upon the elders/shepherding leaders of the assemblies. But unfortunately in many assemblies, they graciously assign this responsibility to others, thus giving an "opportunity" and a "chance" even to many who are not competent to teach the Word. These false ideas emerge from a wrong understanding of the precious doctrine of the priesthood of all believers. As a result the assembly suffers from spiritual malnutrition. Since we have perpetuated a wrong system, it will be a great struggle to undo it.

Ministry and *worship* are different. They are precisely opposite. **Worship** is from men to God, and we all have the privilege and responsibility in worshipping God; in praise, thanksgiving, adoration, and prayers. But many of us fail to exercise our priestly privileges at the Lord's Supper/Worship meeting. In most assemblies, there is a great need for broader participation in the worship meeting. There are also other ample opportunities to serve one another, to witness, and thus exercise our priesthood privileges. **Ministry of the Word** (not just sharing or testimony), on the other hand, is the truth of God which comes from God to man, expounded doctrinally and practically by **gifted men** in the assembly in the power of the Holy Spirit for the edification of the entire church.   This is an area where we need to make lot of changes with a sense of urgency. *Most evangelical churches around us are doing a commendable job in this area.* How quick we are to criticize them in simple matters, when we have totally messed up our pulpit ministries, which should be in the hands of gifted men to minister the Word and edify the people of God. People have even left our assemblies because of the lack of good edifying Word ministry. There was a time when other churches used to flock to the Brethren gatherings for the faithful and effective exposition of the Word. But in many places today Brethren young people go to other churches to hear good Bible exposition.

Edification of the church is the goal of ministry. Only those who have the "speaking gifts" should teach/preach in the assembly during the "ministry time" when the whole congregation assembles to hear the Word of God. This is a very responsible and solemn function. In 1 Cor.14:26, in relation to the participation in the "open" meeting, the emphasis is on **utterance gifts** (teaching, revelation, tongues, and interpretation). When we get up and teach, we are claiming that we have the gift of teaching. Let us be very careful not to make a claim which cannot be justified. There may be appropriate occasions when spiritual believers with less ability may also minister in the assembly. I am not advocating an absolute prohibition or despising of the spiritual contribution of others. But that should not be the *norm* for the ministry of the Word, as it is practiced in most assemblies to our peril. Our freedom is to be exercised with responsibility and accountability.

Equality in priesthood does not imply equality in spiritual gifts. *Let us get this straight: ministry of the word should be by different men, but at the same time by **gifted men***. Priesthood of the believers does not mean "preacherhood" of believers. This is a forgotten truth that needs to be rediscovered in the assemblies.

Let us uphold the glorious doctrine of the priesthood of believers and practice it in integrity. Let us not trivialize its meaning with individualism and wrong practices, and traditions. Since this

80

doctrine is the barometer of our life together in the body of Christ and our testimony in the world, we need more in-depth teaching of it in the assemblies. One senior and respected brother with whom I discussed this matter, exclaimed to me that in this area, we have erred to such an extent that we have gone on an *irreversible* course! I hope this is not true.

"But you are a chosen race, a royal priesthood, a holy nation, a people for God's own possession, that you may proclaim the excellencies of Him who has called you out of darkness into His marvelous light" *(1Peter 2:9).*

9
Plurality of Elders

"And from Miletus he sent to Ephesus and called to him the elders of the church" (Acts 20:17)

The Brethren believe in local church leadership. We believe that a plurality of elders in the local church is most consistent with biblical teaching. The New Testament presents clear evidence that the care of the church was committed to a team of *elders* (in the plural) whom God raised up from within the congregation. These elders are not humanly appointed, neither are they hired through an agency or placement service. The assembly recognizes those whom the Holy Spirit has appointed.

One-man leadership in the church of God is contrary to the teaching of the New Testament. There is an increasing emphasis and recognition on the principle of plurality of leaders/elders/pastors in several evangelical churches today. This is not surprising as anyone who searches the Scripture finds this to be the **norm** (Acts 14:23; 20:17, 28; Phili.1:1; 1 Thess.5:12; Heb.13:17; Jam.5:14; 1Pet. 5:1-3).

The church leaders in the New Testament are consistently called "elders." **There is no**

reference in the New Testament to a "one-pastor" congregation. Why should we even consider a *flexible-form* church government as advocated by some theologians (Flexible form - no standard form or clear pattern of church government is given in the NT. So there can be flexibility and fluidity in church government today) when we have the *normative pattern* clearly given in the New Testament.

Pastor (shepherd) in Eph.4:11 is a *gift* given to the church, and *not* the *title* of the leader of a church as it is commonly used in churches these days. The work of a pastor is *shepherding*. The three terms **"elders," "overseers"** ("bishops"), and **"shepherds"** ("pastors") are interchangeably used in the New Testament (Acts 20:17, 28; 1 Peter 5:1-2). "Elders" are to be "pastors" – "I exhort the elders among you, as your fellow elder......shepherd the flock of God among you" (1 Peter 5:1-2). *Elder* denotes the **dignity and spiritual maturity** of the office; *overseer* designates the **spiritual work** and *pastor* denotes the **spiritual capacity** (the spiritual gift to do the work as a shepherd). Elders as under-shepherds are directly accountable to the Great Shepherd of the sheep, the Lord Jesus Christ.

Biblical eldership is both *plural* and *pastoral*. Elders, dare to be shepherds – "Therefore, I exhort the elders among you, as your fellow elder......shepherd the flock of God" (1 Peter 5:1-2). Each individual member of the church has a personal obligation to be engaged in shepherding

83

ministry to others. When the elders are commanded to shepherd the flock of God, it points to their corporate function rather than to an individual activity.

The Appointment & Recognition of Elders

(For a more detailed discussion of this topic and other leadership issues, you may refer to the author's book, Biblical Principles of Leadership, Gospel Literature Service, India, 2013; also Alexander Strauch, Biblical Eldership, Lewis and Roth Publishers, 1986, 1988).

Questions are frequently asked about the appointment and recognition of elders in the assemblies. To some extent, there is confusion in this matter in the minds of many believers. Clear teaching and some helpful practical guidelines in this regard is much needed. I have heard some Bible teachers presenting the matter of *recognition* as something shrouded in mystery, or they paint it with "ultra-spiritual theories" without any clarity and practical relevance. We don't have to make this sound mystical.

First of all, let us be clear that no specific appointment method is spelled out in the New Testament. This means we have **freedom** in this matter (without violating general Scriptural principles). If this was a matter of utmost significance, the Word of God would have shed considerable light on this matter and have given us specific guidelines. The *form* and *method* of selection is secondary to the elders' *qualification* and *function*.

There are two sides to the question of the appointment of elders – a divine side and a human side. The basic principle is clear in **Acts 20:28**: *the Holy Spirit appoints* (divine side).They are not *elected* by the congregation or the existing elders. We recognize whom the Holy Spirit appoints over us. Man is only to recognize what God has indicated. Appointment and recognition of elders should be solely based on the qualifications and proven commitment of a person to the shepherding work of the local church. *We should recognize those who exhibit the biblical qualifications and are already doing the work required.*

During the apostolic period, elders were appointed by the apostles and their delegates (Acts 14:23; 1 Tim.5:22; Titus 1:5). Since we do not have apostles today, on the basis of the qualifications of elders, the assembly should be able to recognize those men who meet God's requirement. For this to happen, the assembly must be well-taught on these matters. This cannot take place in a vacuum. On a practical level, the **existing elders** as spiritual guides of the assembly (in some cases pioneer missionaries or evangelists) are the ones to take the initiative in this process, involving the assembly. They should prayerfully look out for men who meet the Scriptural qualifications and who are committed to pastoral ministry. It is difficult to delineate hard and fast rules in this matter. "Consecrated common sense", discernment, Scriptural guidelines, prayer, and total dependence on the Lord should guide us in our decision. *Yes, we are able to discern that a man is an elder just as we recognize an individual is gifted to teach.*

Public Recognition

Since elders are the spiritual leaders of the church, they must be **publicly** and **officially** recognized before the assembly. Elders should be known by the assembly, not simply by their names, but by practical recognition (human side) and submission to their pastoral leadership (1 Thess.5:12; 1 Cor.16:15-18). Public recognition is important so that the churches should have no doubt who they are. In some assemblies, there is great reservation in publicly recognizing the elders (in the name of anti-clericalism, sometimes we are hesitant to do necessary things that are helpful to the assembly!).

Strauch's counsel in this regard is insightful: "Official appointment by the acknowledged leadership was necessary because of the elders' and deacons' highly responsible and delicate work on behalf of the congregation. Official appointment greatly facilitated their effectiveness, helped avoid confusion and infighting, and added a greater sense of accountability" (Alexander Strauch, *Biblical Eldership*, 77).

How do we publicly recognize an elder? Again, there are no strict rules that are spelled out in the New Testament. The simplest way we can do it may be through an announcement and a prayer of commendation. *Laying on of hands* is not commanded in Scripture. It is prone to misunderstanding and confusion as it is practiced ceremonially and ritualistically in Christendom today. That is one reason the assemblies tend to avoid it altogether.

I believe there is an appropriate use of laying on of hands in recognizing people who are set apart for special ministries. There is Scriptural precedence for this. This can be a very meaningful expression (without any significance of ecclesiastical ordination, ceremonialism, or ministerial character) of our fellowship, identification, support, and solidarity with their calling and ministry. In Acts 13:1-3, it was a solemn and special act of identification and fellowship in the special missionary service to which the Lord had called His servants (see also Acts 6:1-6). I wonder whether we overreact to certain wrong denominational ceremonies, and totally do away with *simple and meaningful practices* which can be legitimately done, if we desire to do so.

In Acts 14:23 we do not read that the apostles laid their hands on the elders they appointed. But they prayed with fasting. It is a golden rule for all of us to follow. But in 1Tim.5:22, as Paul instructed Timothy concerning elders he was told not to "lay hands on anyone too hastily." It implies the *public recognition and identification with a person by the act of laying hands on him.*

Though we always oppose denominational and ceremonial practices, it is surprising that other unscriptural procedures in relation to leadership are easily accommodated in some assemblies – elders are recognized on the basis of their seniority as members, their age, secular and financial status, the merit of being a founding member of the assembly, family influence, favoritism etc. None of these are the criteria for eldership. There is no Scripture to support all these wrong practices. This trend has created a leadership vacuum in many assemblies (and as we all know, it is a BIG VACUUM!). We must be governed by *simplicity* and *spirituality*. When spiritual and Scriptural qualifications are neglected, the result will be disastrous. This is the primary reason for **leadership crisis** which we find today. This should be a matter of concern and earnest prayer. Leaders with "integrity of heart and skillfulness of hands" (Psalm 78:72), and "men who understood the times and with knowledge of what [people] should do" (1 Chro.12:32) is the need of the hour.

Should Elders Serve for Life?

This is another frequently asked question. How long shall an elder serve in a church? The length of term for the elders is nowhere stated in the New Testament. We cannot rigidly put a time limit on what is a calling by God to one of the offices of the church. But at the same time, we should not make this an excuse for a "life-time elder" even if the person is *not* capable of discharging the duties of eldership.

Elders can serve as long as they are biblically qualified and are able to function effectively in carrying out their pastoral duties. When they are not able to carry out their work due to age, health, family or personal reasons, they must willingly step aside and pass on the responsibility to others. The false doctrine of "elder for lifetime" ("once an elder, always an elder") has ruined the blessing and growth of many assemblies (Usually a "spiritual" and "pious" excuse is given to cling on to their position: "leadership is not an employment and hence there is no retirement!"). **Only active elders are *elders*.** This writer does not support the idea of retaining the title "elder" for an individual even after his service in the church as an elder.

Full-Time Elders

Most of the assemblies do not have full time elders, though we have many full-time evangelists, itinerant preachers and teachers of the Word. As far as I know, the idea of full-time elders is seldom discussed, prayed for, or encouraged in most assemblies, though most of us may not be opposed to it in theory. It is true that many of the elders in the assemblies do a commendable job for the church with great sacrifice, working hard with their own hands to meet their material needs. Thus they labor for the Lord faithfully without becoming a burden for the assembly. In most churches who follow a "pastor" system, they have at least one full-time pastor and then several "lay elders" who may have secular employment along with their ministry responsibilities.

In a fast-paced, busy world in which we live, along with the various challenges facing us every day, both at work and at home, there are a lot of factors that can make things harder. An elder's responsibilities at work, home, and church create **a real time crunch. This is an undeniable fact and no theology can do away with it**. As a result, the priority for pastoral care will diminish (and generally speaking it has diminished in many assemblies). However an elder tries and adjusts his schedule, the time allocated for shepherding will suffer. The time crunch can adversely affect his preparation, study, prayer, and other spiritual disciplines also. These pressures can create a lot of tension for him and also his family. This practical problem has nothing to do with the elders' sincerity, commitment, or honesty; it is simply the reality of life. It is high time we face this truth.

In spite of all the pressures and limitations of life, we praise God for our elders who strive to do a *glorious work* in their shepherding ministry. **But we need something more.** I believe the time has come for assemblies to think more seriously about encouraging some of our elders (at least one elder in each assembly) to be in *full-time* service. There are some assemblies who practice this model. In such assemblies, there is meaningful pastoral care, growth and blessing (We should not forget that the Charismatic/Pentecostal churches attract lot of people to their fold, not through their doctrine, but by caring pastoral ministry). Let us not *spiritualize* or *theologize* our failure in this matter, but try to do something about it. *I believe this is the most urgent need in the assemblies today*. Let us humbly and honestly acknowledge the fact that we lag behind in our *pastoral care* and ask the Lord to help us in this area of ministry. We need to reinstate the terms "pastor" and "pastoral care" in its *Scriptural sense* in our vocabulary. We cannot let the bleeding and wounded sheep suffer for too long, lest they go after other shepherds.

When we have full time elders, we have an obligation to **support them financially**. The policy, philosophy, and methodology of support must be sorted out by each assembly. It seems that in the early church, some elders were financially supported by the church for their labor in the assembly. **1 Tim.5:17-18** indicates that the church was beginning to face the question of financial support of its elders. In the light of the context and the verses quoted by Paul (Deut.25:4; Luke 10:7), he was encouraging the **financial support of elders** (see the word "honor" used in 1 Tim.5:3 and in Jesus's words in Matt.15:3-6; material and financial support is implied). In 1 Cori.9:1-14 and Gal. 6:6 also, Paul writes about material support.

Some of us seem to be quite biased to the regular support idea and they expend all their energy to prove that "honor" in 1 Tim.5 does not mean financial support. This is a vain attempt. Some of them may lean towards the "support" idea, but are very much against if the support is "regular." It may be an overreaction to the wrong practices in many denominations. We do not conclude that the elders in the New Testament churches were "paid" for their service. Assemblies do not "hire" anyone on a salaried basis for ministry. We do not receive a salary for serving the Lord.

The important matter here is not the "pay" but our willingness to cheerfully "support" those who deserve it. It is a spiritually unhealthy trend to spend all your time earning a living, and then use the "spare time" (if you have any!) to shepherd the flock of God. No wonder this theology has weakened the assemblies considerably. Yes, this writer believes that "full time workers/elders" are indispensable for effective pastoral ministry in the assemblies today. Being supported financially give the worker extra time (not extra status) to serve the Lord and His people. The idea of "support" should not be construed always as "paid" employment type of ministry.

For us to meaningfully implement this practice of regular support for full-time elders (and also for evangelists), we need a revision of our "extreme theology" that the full-time workers (evangelists, missionaries or elders) are to "live by faith." What about other believers? *Did we forget the fact that all children of God have to live by faith?*

We do not believe or encourage a "salaried employment" type of ministry. We see the Lord's work very different from secular work. The Gospel of Christ must be made available without charge (1 Cor.9:16-18). Pastoral ministry should not be done for sordid gain (1 Pet.5:2: "filthy lucre," KJV). At the same time, those who faithfully serve the Lord without a regular income from a salary or other means, must be responsibly supported regularly, since they also have daily expenses and needs like others. How foolishly we have cherished a wrong theology that regular support is wrong! But we only apply this to full-time workers and missionaries! All other believers can have a regular salary (even work overtime!) and they depend on it!

What we call the "support" is not the important issue. When we have regular needs, we need regular support. All of us live and operate on this basis. The need and desire for a set income on a regular basis, should not be interpreted as having no faith. We cannot validate such immature thinking scripturally. This is another area where we need to think more practically and scripturally, willing to revise our theology of "support". There is no need of any inflexible dogmatism in this matter. None of the things discussed here is against our basic theology of "faith ministry".

The Lord meets the needs of His servants through the people of God. The servant looks to the Lord for his needs, and the Lord looks to His people to meet those needs in a practical and caring way. The primary responsibility falls on the commending or local assembly. Since the Lord is no man's debtor, He may use other means and methods to supply the temporal needs of the workers. The Lord's business is to take care of those who look after His business. He will definitely reward them for their labors in His vineyard. But we should not take this as an excuse to think lightly of our responsibility, or to promote an idea that cannot be defended either by Scripture or common sense.

It is high time that we develop a Scriptural vision for effective pastoral leadership in local assemblies. The lack of spiritually mature and able men to lead the assemblies have contributed immensely to the decline of the assemblies. When it comes to leadership issues, it is very vague and obscure in many assemblies. The sheep suffer without shepherds to lead and feed them.

Trained Leadership

The call for more pastoral care ministries among us, bring us to another neglected area - the need for *trained elders*. It does not necessarily mean academically trained elders, but at least we need shepherds who are authentically knowledgeable in the Word and in the various dynamics of pastoral ministries in the contemporary life-situations, and who are equipped to minister effectively as shepherds. This is not a call to "professionalize" ministry, but a challenge to "be diligent to present yourself approved to God as a workman who does not need to be ashamed, handling accurately the word of truth" (2 Tim 2:15).

In relation to missions and evangelism, assemblies and assembly organizations are providing basic training for missionaries. Even in other areas of ministries, there is more openness for the idea of some kind of training. But when it comes to the shepherding task, which is one of the most vital responsibilities of the assembly, generally speaking, there is no emphasis, encouragement, or openness to the need for some kind of training (even within the local assemblies). This writer believes that this is a great deficiency that needs to be urgently addressed for the health and benefit of the assemblies.

It is usually alleged that spiritual pride can arise when training, learning, talents, gifts and abilities become the standards of ministry. Of course, none of these things should be the determining factors in ministry. But we must not forget the fact that spiritual pride can occur without any of these things (and even from the lack of these things). Professionalism can lead to disaster, and in the same way, lack of knowledge and training can even lead to greater disasters, as it is evidenced in many assemblies. "Ignorance is bliss" is not a helpful attitude in ministry (my father who was a self-learned man used to remind us that God never places a premium on ignorance as many people think). Instead of denigrating the value of training or coaching, we need to encourage it more, though in the assemblies we do not make it an essential requirement for ministry. Theological education in its right sense can better equip us to serve. The goal of the gift of teaching is to edify the congregation and equip every saint for the work of ministry (Eph.4:12).

Let us not forget that some of the early Brethren were intellectual giants, and men of great learning, well trained in various secular disciplines, Bible, and theology. But they were spiritual, humble, and godly. Scholarship and godliness embraced each other in their life and ministry. Trained and learned men should not be despised if they are sound in the Word and pure in life. The same standard also applies to untrained men. There were several untrained men mighty in the Scriptures in the history of the assemblies. But they were all disciplined and diligent students of the Word, laboring in it day and night.

Through diligent and systematic study of the Word, the study of scripturally sound materials on pastoral care, seminars on leadership and pastoral care, sessions of prayer and discussion on pastoral issues, hearing from the experience of other shepherds, are some of the simple, practical means through which we can sharpen our skill in the area of pastoral ministry. If our elders are willing to undergo such basic training, it will revolutionize their shepherding work. "As Iron sharpens iron, so one man sharpens another" (Prov.27:17, NIV).

One of our distinctive emphases is the primacy and priority of the Word of God in Christian life and ministry. The Bible is the guide for every Christian and the source of instruction for his daily life. The exposition and teaching of the Word is central to our gatherings. The pulpit ministry, the educational program, the discipleship program, the youth program, and the evangelistic and missionary program of the church are all rooted upon the teaching, training, and equipping in the Word. This can be done effectively only by called, gifted, and trained leaders in the assembly. We have to be more sensitive to these practical issues and be realistic, rather than just harping on *plurality* alone. *Plurality* is not the only truth related to church leadership.

Mentoring Leadership

Paul believed in mentoring leadership. "And the things which you have heard from me in the presence of many witnesses, these entrust to faithful men, who will be able to teach others also" (2 Tim.2:2). This is a call to find the right persons and equip them for ministry. Even in assemblies where able men have ministered and shepherded for many years, a future generation of leaders is not in view. This is the sad story in many assemblies. Teachers and shepherds have a special responsibility to faithfully teach and equip competent people who can faithfully lead in their generation. There is a great need to passionately follow the biblical vision for leadership development.

But we seldom hear or think about this. If assemblies are to be strong its leaders are to be strong.

Listen to the convicting words of the earliest Brethren historian: "Brethrenism has shown itself lamentably incapable of perpetuating a race of leaders. Its characteristic "haphazardism" (if I may be allowed such a term) comes out in this. No provision has been made for the higher studies connected with theology, and now that the contagious enthusiasm that once drew so many highly trained minds into its ranks has waned. Brethrenism is for the most part bereft of well qualified guides" (William Blair Neatby, *A History Of The Plymouth Brethren,* 338).

May the Lord give us the vision, hunger and thirst for caring for the sheep in a more significant way, in a Scriptural way, in an impacting way, and also in a practical way. At the same time, let us also not forget to be "caring" for the "caregivers".

God's Pattern of Ministry

God's pattern of ministry is outlined in **Eph.4:11-13**. The gifting of Christ includes gifted *leaders* for the church – He gave "some" (not "all") as **evangelists, pastors and teachers** (apostles and prophets have laid the foundation). They are in place for the advancement for the church. They have a *unique and special place* as *equipping leaders* ("for the equipping of the saints") and we should be prepared to accept them and recognize their ministry. Following the pattern revealed to us in the New Testament, we recognize no professional ministry in the church. But we should recognize the ministry of gifted men in the assembly established by the Lord. By rejecting "one-man" ministry, many assemblies have fallen into the trap of "any-man" ministry. This is an area where we need radical reform. The equipping leaders should equip the saints for the work of service. In our zeal for anti-clericalism, we sometimes minimize or even neglect the importance of *equipping* leaders. A team of plural, pastoral and biblically qualified spiritual leadership in shepherding and equipping ministries is an integral part of New Testament ecclesiology (doctrine of the church). By ignoring God's pattern of ministry, a claim for New Testament pattern has no real relevance or validity.

"And He gave some as apostles, and some as prophets, and some as evangelists, and some as pastors and teachers, for the equipping of the saints for the work of service, to the building up of the body of Christ" (Eph.4:11-12).

10
Emphasis on Fellowship, Rather Than Membership

"God is faithful, through whom you were called into fellowship with His Son Jesus Christ our Lord
(1 Cor.1:9)

In the New Testament, *fellowship* ("sharing", "communion") expresses shared participation in Christ and the bond that Christ creates between members of the body of Christ. The bond that links us to Jesus also binds us to one another in fellowship. The unity of the body of Christ and the mutual fellowship between believers in Christ (without denominational barriers) were the hallmarks of the historical beginning of the Brethren movement. Christians who associated with the Brethren movement did not find biblical validity for the rigid, hierarchical, and highly organized denominational membership system prevalent in Christian churches. The Christian church in the New Testament was an active fellowship of loving, sharing, and caring Christians. It is one of four essential activities the early church continued steadfastly (Acts 2:42).

The Brethren were unwilling to identify themselves in any other way than as *believers* in Jesus Christ. They had a great vision, directly derived from the study of Scriptures, of a corporate worldwide witness to the unity of the body of Christ. They had no fascination for the idea of "joining a church" since you are already joined to the church (the Body of Christ) the moment you are joined to the Head of the church (Jesus Christ). All who are "in Christ" are also in the "Church." The church is a body of true believers in Christ, baptized by the Holy Spirit into that body (1 Cor.12:13) and joined to the Lord and to one another. Those who were saved were added to the church by the Lord (Acts 2:47). Those whom He saved He joined to the church by His Spirit. There are many today who may "join" a church or become "members" of a church, but may not belong to the Christ and to the true Church. The idea of "becoming a member of the church" is not found in the New Testament.

Moreover, the church in the New Testament is characterized as a divine *organism*, a living, vibrant, spiritual body and not as an *organization*. Regeneration is the prime requisite for membership in the church. Believers are members of this spiritual organism – the Body of Christ (Rom.12:4-5; Eph.5:30). Assemblies have always emphasized this truth and wanted to be more Scriptural in relation to the question of membership. Our emphasis always has been for *fellowship* in the body of Christ, than membership in any organizational sense.

The emphasis on fellowship does not mean that we are against (or have to be) against all ideas of membership in a local church. Our emphasis on fellowship is not a total denial of some form of membership in a local assembly. The question of membership surfaces only in relation to one's full identification and involvement with a local body of believers. We need balance and thoughtfulness in practicing this distinctive. We need revision and rethinking in applying this distinctive meaningfully and scripturally (some of us may not even consider this to be a distinctive, but some may totally deny any reference to membership).

Most of the assemblies have an address list, or a directory of all those who have identified themselves with that group of believers and those who regularly meet with that assembly. They are *members* of that congregation. This is a sort of *membership* (even if we shy away from that term) for all practical purposes. It does not mean that we have compromised on any doctrine. This practical aspect of responsible fellowship is equivalent to the idea of membership (the term "membership" in the church today in its normal/practical usage is in relation to the local church, and not the universal church). Only when a person is baptized, he/she is received into the full fellowship of the assembly. Full reception, fellowship and involvement in the local assembly naturally brings with it responsibility and accountability. This leads to some form of membership. This is how local assemblies function in order and discipline.

Organization & Membership in the New Testament

Avoiding extremes, and maintaining a balanced perspective is essential in relation to the understanding, appreciation, and application of the biblical distinctives of the assemblies. This is essential in dealing with the issues we are discussing in this book. That is why it is reminded time and again. We have to pay more attention to the application of the doctrines which we believe.

Does the New Testament give any evidence of an organized church? Since the church is a spiritual organism, can we contend that there is no organized structure of the church in the New Testament? While we emphasize fellowship, is there anything wrong to have a membership idea in relation to the local assemblies?

Contrary to the popular notion among us, throughout the New Testament, the **organism is organized** to carry out its ministries, and to maintain order and decorum. Sometimes we totally disregard or ignore such truths to promote a greater sense of "spirituality" of our own. Of course, the organization in the New Testament churches was not done through human ideas for the church to be popular or successful, but it was carried out under the direction of the Holy Spirit. The Word of God lays our approach to organization (we are **not** talking about para-church organization) **within the assembly**. We do not have to be following the methodologies of the world or the unscriptural hierarchical organizational structure of denominations. At the same time we should not ignore the scriptural guidelines related to the *organized* functioning of the *organism*.

The Church, the spiritual organism, is designed to function effectively. As such it is organized, or arranged as a unit to carry out its ministries. The nature and function of the church testifies to the divinely sanctioned organizational arrangement in the assembly. The organism performs its tasks through its organization. From the practices, functions, responsibilities, and ministries, a simple organizational structure is evident in the New Testament churches:

- The churches in the New Testament had offices of elders and deacons (Phil.1:1; Acts 20:17; 14:23). They were to be selected and recognized according to the qualifications specified (1 Tim.3; Titus 1:5-9).
- The Church at Jerusalem enlisted seven men who could care for the widows (Acts 6:1-6).
- The church had the authority to exercise discipline and to judge its own members (1 Cor.5:1-13).
- The church has to settle its own internal problems (1 Cor.6:1-5).

- The regular corporate gathering of the church was commanded (Heb.10:25).
- The believers united in public worship, prayer meeting, and the celebration of the Lord's Supper (Acts 2:41-42; 20:7).
- The meeting of the church had to be conducted decently and in order (1 Cor.14:40).
- The believers knew the number of their members (Acts 2:41; 4:4).
- Letters of commendation were sent from one church to another (2 Cor.3:1; Acts 18:24-28).
- Churches had a treasury. Collections were taken regularly and sent to take care of the poor and needy (1 Cor.16:1-2; 2Cor.8-9; Rom.15:26). Churches were also encouraged to support its workers (1Tim.5:17).
- Churches kept registers of the widows under their care – "let a widow be put on the list...." (1 Tim.5:9).

One wonders how these ministries and functions can be carried out decently and in order, without some basic organization within the assembly. How can we ignore such valuable information that are clearly recorded in the pages of the New Testament?

In a doctrinal sense, church *membership is* associated with the Body of Christ and church *fellowship* with the local church. The local church gathers as the body of Christ and is representative of it. In the local church, we receive one another as Christ also received us. Only those who are members of Christ's body through faith in Christ (personal salvation experience) can be scripturally received into fellowship with the local church. The idea of *membership* in a local church is actually an extension of the concept of **responsible fellowship** in the local church. Christian life does not stop with the blessing of being called into fellowship with God and made a member of the body of Christ. It is more than a demonstration of our unity. Bond of fellowship brings in responsibilities for the believer, both to give himself to the Lord and to fellow believers. It also involves sharing in the total life and ministries of the assembly. These practical aspects of fellowship cannot be overlooked or deemphasized.

To facilitate responsible and accountable service with a group of believers in a given location, one has to have a recognized relationship and involvement with that group, which amounts to some sort of *membership*. It also helps people to submit to the spiritual leadership of a local assembly in a responsible way (Heb.13:17). If a believer does not belong to a local church (member of a local assembly), then to which leaders does an individual

Christian obey and submit to? For which flock do the elders/shepherds give account for? The shepherds should know *who* the sheep God has given them are. A sense of belonging to a particular gathering of believers in a locality in a consistent manner is essential to foster meaningful fellowship, service, and pastoral care. "Free-floating" Christian life is not in in the plan and purpose of God.

Most of the observations mentioned above for the organizational nature of the church also argue for the evidence of church membership. Throughout the Book of Acts, there is a numerical record of those who have professed faith in Christ and were joined to the church (2:41, 47; 4:4; 5:14; 6:1, 7; 11:21; 16:5; 17:12 etc.). It seems that somebody was tracking the growth. *Quantitative* as well as *qualitative* church growth is recorded in the book of Acts. The list of widows (1 Tim. 5), the selection of seven men to address a specific problem in the Jerusalem Church (Acts 6), letters of commendation (2 Cor.3), church discipline (1 Cor.5), all point towards responsible membership in the early church. Without some kind of membership, how can the church excommunicate one of its members?

Yes, we emphasize fellowship more than membership - the truth of fellowship in the church because of membership in the Body of Christ through faith in Christ. We do not follow or subscribe to an elaborate membership process or rituals that are practiced in many denominations. *However, local church membership in its true sense is a commitment to a particular body of believers, and what they stand for, and their submission to the leadership of that church, and also their willingness to serve the Lord in that company of believers.* This is where we will primarily use and develop the spiritual gifts the Lord has given to each member of the body. Let us remember that the body analogy of the church has one global (Ephesians and Colossians) and local (1Corinthians) meaning. *There is no commandment to be a local church member, but it is implied in the nature and function of the church.*

Our practices for church life should be regulated by the Word of God. We do not have to come up with our own ideas. When Scripture does not speak directly to something, we need some standard to judge how to apply some models and examples in the Scripture. There is no command or requirement in the Word to implement membership in the local assembly. But it is something that is good, necessary and useful for the responsible function and smooth operation of the local assembly. We find that model in the New Testament. When no clear **precept** is available to us, we have to follow the apostolic **practice**. We do that in many other areas of assembly life. Knowingly or unknowingly, acknowledging or not acknowledging, we all practice some sort of membership in most assemblies. Without it, we will be non-functional. As in other areas of our practice, here also we need balance, and should avoid extremes.

"For what have I to do with judging outsiders? Do you not judge those who are within the church" (1Cor.6:12)?

11
Weekly Observance of The Lord's Supper

"Do this in remembrance of Me" (Luke 22:19)

Luke describes the life in the early church by telling us that the believers in it were distinguished by their devotion to the "apostles' teaching and to fellowship, to the breaking of bread and to prayer" (Acts 2:42). These four elements mentioned here are still the basic parts of the life of the church. We can call them the **"four pillars of the church."** "The breaking of bread" is a reference to the observance of the Lord's Supper.

The Brethren assemblies are committed to a regular, weekly celebration of the Lord's Supper. This can be considered as the most cherished distinctive of the Brethren assemblies. The Lord's Supper is an ordinance which evokes worship and it is an integral part of the "meeting" of the church. The worship of God's people finds high expression through the ordinance of the Lord's Supper. It was a vital part of the weekly gathering of the Lord's people in the early church (Acts 2:42; 20:7). The "breaking of bread" meeting has always been something very dear to the Brethren throughout their history.

111

Most of the evangelical churches in our time are not devoted to a regular observance of the Lord's Supper, though most of them acknowledge the significance of it in the life of the church. The usual practice is to observe it monthly, quarterly, semi-annually, annually, and on special days like Easter or Christmas. In some churches, even when it is observed, it is given little emphasis. Others relegate it to a smaller midweek optional service, and in many other churches, it is appended to a preaching service, hurriedly done with no major significance. There are other churches that observe it periodically with due reverence and importance.

The regular observance of the Lord's Supper will not easily fit into the mold of the "seeker sensitive" churches. In a "user-friendly" environment "relevance" is more important than "remembrance" (and also "reverence"). The opinion expressed by J. Van Bruggen (a minister of the Reformed Churches of Netherlands) comes to mind: "Our infrequent celebration of the Lord's Supper is evidence of a low level spiritual life."

The Frequency of the Lord's Supper

There is no specific instruction or command in the New Testament on *how often* the Lord's Supper is to be observed. **Acts 20:7** suggests that it was observed *regularly* on the first day of the week. A more frequent observance is indicated in **Acts 2:46**. The **regular** observance of the Lord's Supper was one of the foundational practices of the early church (**Acts 2:42**). The early Christians met together on the first day of every week for corporate worship (**1 Cor.16:2**). Paul instructs in **1 Cor.11:26**: "For as often as you eat this bread and drink this cup...." "**As often as**" definitely indicates frequency. Paul does not say "as seldom" or "as often as you may choose." Though Paul gives no directions as to how frequently the Lord's Supper is to be observed, he implies that it is to be done frequently.

From the overall evidence the New Testament presents, "as often as" refers to every time the church came together for corporate worship (note the repeated usage of the phrase "come together" in 1 Cor.11:17, 18, 20, 33, 34; 14: 23, 26). Paul assumes that the Corinthian church would celebrate the Lord's Supper every time they come together as church" (1 Cor.11:18). In this very letter, Paul indicates that they come together as church once each week, on the first day of the week. He encourages them to set money aside – Christian giving is to be done regularly on Sunday (I enjoy considering "Sunday" as "SONday"). It is evident from **1 Cor.11** and **16** when the church comes together their service included **at least two items: celebration of the Lord's Supper and collection of money**. As Gibbs observes, "Those who object to the weekly observance of the Lord's Supper certainly have no objection to taking a collection each first day of the week! If it is true of the one, it is also true of the other" (Alfred P. Gibbs, *The Lord's Supper*, Walterick Publishers, 1963, 183).

It is an established fact that the "communion service" was an integral part of the early Christian worship. This is also supported by the testimony of early church history. *Didache*, the earliest writing after the New Testament (between A.D. 90—120) states that the Lord's Supper was celebrated weekly on the Lord's Day. The early Church fathers Ignatius (born between A.D.35-50 and died between A. D. 98-117), Justin Martyr (A.D.110-165), and Irenaus (A.D.120 - 202) all attest to the fact of the weekly celebration of the Lord's Supper. This practice and example which we see in Acts 2 (Jerusalem), 20 (Troas), and 1Cor.11 (Corinth) became the pattern throughout the churches.

The observance of the Lord's Supper weekly in the Brethren assemblies *is not out of a biblical command, but out of biblical pattern, practice, and principle*. All the available evidence in the New Testament directs to a frequent (weekly) observance of the ordinance of the Lord's Supper. The established order in the early church is clear: on the first day of the week the church came together to celebrate the ordinance of the Lord's Supper. We delight to do in like manner (we acknowledge that there are other Christian congregations also who regularly observe the Lord's Supper). Where there is no clear apostolic *precept*, we follow the apostolic *practice*. God's approval and authority is revealed to us by practices, examples, patterns, and necessary inferences, as well as by direct commands.

It may be startling news for many evangelicals to know that many revered Christian leaders of the past including Luther, Calvin, Wesley, and Spurgeon argued for a weekly observance of the Lord's Supper (David Dunlap in his book, *His Dying Request*, Bible & Life Ministries, Inc., 2006, has compiled the classic writings and sermons of evangelical leaders, both past and present, on the importance of the regular observance of the Lord's Supper. I highly recommend it to the readers). It is surprising that even the World Council of Churches (theologically "liberal" to the core) in a document called *Baptism, Eucharist and Ministry* (1982), made a recommendation on the frequency of the Lord's Supper. Even they could not overlook the Scriptural evidence for its frequency! It was a shock to the member churches, as the vast majority of them do not observe the Lord's Supper weekly.

Some denominations think that familiarity will diminish the meaning of the ordinance ("sacrament" to some), thereby weakening faith. They argue that frequent observance of the Lord's Supper will make it seem trivial, casual, and commonplace (yes, we have to guard against this danger). If we apply the same logic to prayer, worship, "quiet time" and other Christian disciplines, the result will be disastrous. Usually, the reluctance to observe it frequently stems from "practical reasons" (large church setting, not enough time to observe it every Sunday, denominational precedence, superstitious ceremonialism etc.). Some Christians argue that the infrequent observance can make the Lord's Supper something very "special". The way to make something special is by cherishing it, not by reducing the frequency. Reducing the frequency only makes it *infrequent* and not *special*! Others argue that the frequency of the Lord's Supper is not a question of biblical necessity, but is a circumstance that is to be determined by the particular local church. Thus goes all the excuses of the churches....

But all these so-called "reasons" (or excuses?) seem to be shallow and empty when the Bible places high significance on the **frequent** observance of the Lord's Supper. This is what the Lord expects from His people. It is the Lord's desire that His people often remember His death in this way. Without doubt this is what the early church did. God's people have enjoyed the blessings of frequently observing it throughout the history of the Christian Church. If we desire conformity to the apostolic pattern, we have to give the Lord's Supper its recognized place. Our worship finds high expression through this "feast of remembrance" – remembering the one "who remembered us in our low estate". It is to be a continuing practice of the Christian Church.

Points to Ponder

From a very practical and realistic perspective, I believe a word of caution is not out of place. Sometimes we develop a mindset which promotes spiritual pride in us by "looking down" upon other Christians who may *not* be observing the Lord's Supper every week, though they may have so many other Scriptural characteristics and elements in their gathering (and we may be missing several of them!). We must acknowledge that many believers, who have not seen some of the precious truths we hold on to, may be more fervent in their love and devotion to the Lord. We don't have to make any compromise on our convictions, but let us not think that since we observe the Lord's Supper weekly, that places us on a higher spiritual pedestal. Remember, we also have to learn many valuable spiritual practices from others.

Sometimes many of us are tempted to cherish a "feel good theology" of our own, that since we observe the Lord's Supper every week, that's all we need even if other vital elements in church life are missing. How reluctant we become to acknowledge the biblical traits and examples in other Christians, which will be of tremendous value to us if we follow it! Let us not forget that we may be missing out on other areas of the "four pillars" of the church (Acts 2:42) like systematic teaching of the Word (missing in most assemblies today), dynamic Christian fellowship, and inspiring prayer services (just think about the mid-week prayer meetings in most assemblies!). By emphasizing one, let us not abandon the significance of other vital Christian experiences that are an integral part of New Testament pattern. Just by clinging on to the regular observance of the Lord's Supper, no assembly automatically becomes New Testament pattern.

A Sacred Observance

When we come to worship the one who is "Holy and Reverend," our attitude should be characterized by "reverence and godly fear." Though we do not subscribe to a "sacramental theology" of the Lord's Supper, and do not attach any ceremony to it, it is imperative that we should consider it as a very sacred observance. Familiarity and frequency should not breed a casual attitude in the observance, decorum, dignity, at the administering of the Lord's Supper. Those who administer it also should be considerate of these matters. Our freedom should not lead to the point of disorder and irreverence (1 Cor.14:26).

Brian Gunning warns on the danger of familiarity when he writes:

"Some behavior is out of place in the presence of God. The holiness of God is not intended to immobilize us in fear, but neither should we be casual in our conduct in assembly meetings. To be continually late, to dress sloppily, seems to make a statement about how we value our meeting with Him. To be cavalier or silly in our public expression, or to fill our platform ministry with talk about ourselves, exposes our small thoughts of God. How did the disciples speak of Him? The New Testament will tell you" (*Danger*, Uplook, October, 1999).

The honor and dignity of the occasion should be maintained each time we observe the Lord's Supper. This is a matter of solemn importance as Paul's own words in 1 Cor.11:23-34 remind us. The seriousness of the symbol must be kept in mind as we gather around the Lord's Table. It is not to be taken lightly. Sickness and even death were two consequences for those who had approached the Lord's Table in a careless and sinful manner (1 Cor.11:27-30). Taking into consideration all the spiritual realities represented by the Lord's Supper, it is indeed a very sacred observance and it has to be maintained that way. A "symbolic view" of the Lord's Supper also should not diminish our reverence for it (Chapters 19, 20, and 21 of A.P. Gibb's book, *The Lord's Supper* addresses some of the practical issues of reverence, responsibility, and preparation in relation to the Lord's Supper. These chapters are good materials to be taught in the assemblies with discussion).

Reception at the Lord's Supper

The Lord's Supper is for *believers only*. Believers in the Lord Jesus Christ who are doctrinally sound (essential/fundamental truths of the faith), and morally clean are to be received at the Lord's Supper. The privilege to participate in it is open to "those who have been sanctified in Christ Jesus, saints by calling, with all who in every place call upon the name of our Lord Jesus Christ, their Lord and ours" (1 Cor.1:2). The reception of a believer is in the name of Christ, not on any other ground. We should receive all whom God has received.

To the early Brethren, "gathering unto the name of the Lord Jesus Christ" was a way of expressing one's identity with the whole Body of Christ, irrespective of denominational labels. The Lord's Supper was seen as a symbol of the unity of all who belonged to Christ. This was a uniquely distinctive trait of the Brethren, as this is the clear teaching of the Word of God. They received all Christians at the Lord's Supper who were sound in doctrine and life. Our fellowship with the Triune God becomes the basis of our fellowship with God's people. All true believers called into the fellowship of the Son should be welcomed into the fellowship of God's people, unless debarred by unclean lives or unsound doctrine (1Cor.5:11; Tit.1:13; 3:10-11; 2Thess.3:6, 14). There is no warrant in the Word of God for imposing any further restrictions whatsoever. "Accept one another, then, just as Christ accepted you" (Rom.15:7, NIV). **Now this does not mean** a general and open invitation to any and everyone in the assembled company to freely partake of the Lord's Supper. Scriptural guidelines and restrictions are to be followed always.

The Lord's Supper is not a denominational ritual. It belongs to the *Lord*. By its very nature, it is the communion of the body and blood of Christ, and it is meant for all those who have a share in Him and His salvation blessings. It expresses the fellowship ("sharing," "participation") of believers in the body of Christ (1Cor.10:16-17). It is communing with the Lord and with His people, and a profound celebration of our common salvation and eternal life. How can anyone impose denominational or sectarian barriers and legalistic restrictions on this solemn ordinance? Such practices are against the Scripture and also against the true Brethren ideal.

It is quite unfortunate that some Brethren have distorted the Scriptural emphasis of fellowship and reception at the Lord's Table. Those who speak eloquently against sectarianism become "sectarian" to the core in relation to the question of reception. It is done on party lines, and the emphasis has shifted from "life" to "light," from "unity" to "uniformity." To them, "gathered in the name of the Lord Jesus" has become another sectarian or denominational expression. The reception is extended *only* to those who hold the "exact right doctrine in every details of the faith." They have their own definition of "fellowship" to support their rigidity. Believers are "examined" (very stringent legalistic laws of commendation letter is also applied in some instances) to see whether they meet **all** the sectarian and legalistic criteria before they are welcomed into the Lord's Table. Sometimes faulty exegesis and doctrinal gymnastics are paraded to justify this attitude. You may find this even in some of our Bible commentaries and books. What a departure from the Scripture and the true Brethren spirit!

The words of a prominent Brethren scholar throw much light on the issues of reception, fellowship, and the Lord's Table:

"Apart from cases of false teaching and immorality, the adoption of rigid regulations is precarious.......What is needed is watchfulness and care on the part of those who are appointed to exercise oversight – watchfulness against the reception of those whose life or teaching is inconsistent with the gospel, and those who give evidence of being such as to cause division. To go beyond this is to usurp the authority of Christ" (W.E. Vine, *The Church and The Churches*, Chapter 15: "Reception," www.a wilderness voice.com/Church &Churches).

Vine further writes in the same chapter:

".....Fellowship is not conditioned upon the measure of light received. Deficiency of spiritual understanding in this respect affords no reason for the rejection of one who is a member of the body of Christ and walking in godliness of life. Reception of such does not involve carelessness or looseness in doctrine or in the fulfillment of God's will."

A profound statement of C. F. Hogg is quoted by F.F. Bruce:

"C.F. Hogg used to say that a sect is formed when we put a limiting adjective before the word 'Christian' or any other word that embraces all the people of God, in order to distinguish some of them ecclesiastically from others. A simple way of finding out whether a church is a sect or not is to inquire whether it imposes any condition for admitting believers to its fellowship over and above those which Christ has required for receiving them to fellowship with Himself" (*Answers To Questions*, Paternoster, 1973, 241).

As we regularly observe the Lord's Supper, let us realize and appreciate its true meaning, and remember that this is a very precious ordinance instituted by the Son of God, on the eve of His substitutionary death on the cross. Let us continue to worship and remember Him in His own appointed way.

Open & Spontaneous Worship

Though we do not know *how* exactly the early church conducted its worship meeting, from 1 Cor. 11-14 we get an intimate glimpse of the early church at worship. Here we find the assembly gathered (11-17-14:40) together for the observance of the Lord's Supper and other spiritual activities, energized, directed and controlled by the Spirit of God (*Pneumatic Christianity*, if I may use a term popular in the Charismatic circles). It seems that it was an "open" meeting, dynamic and unstructured, without any settled format, and was informal and free. This is the impression one gets reading **1 Cor.14:26**: "What is the outcome then, brethren? When you assemble, each one has a psalm, has a teaching, has a revelation, has a tongue, has an interpretation. Let all things be done for edification." "Free participation in the service is indicated by this verse, but not to the point of disorder" (Ryrie Study Bible, NASB, 1978, 1746). The *principles* are valid in the assembly gatherings today despite the cessation of sign (miraculous) gifts. This is the pattern we try to follow in the meeting of the church on Sundays, and this pattern is biblically defensible and this is the only pattern presented in the New Testament.

It is important for us to observe that pastors, evangelists, elders, or deacons are *no*t mentioned in the context of this meeting at all. There was no professional clergy controlling or presiding the meeting, or conducting the services. There is spontaneity and freedom, and no settled format. The people of God draw near to His holy presence and can exercise the privilege and responsibility of the priesthood. It was a meeting superintended by the Holy Spirit.

Commenting on 1 Cor.14:26-33, The Church of Scotland minister and Bible commentator William Barclay (who was a "liberal evangelical") writes: "There is no more interesting section in the whole letter than this, for it sheds a flood of light on what an early church service was like. There was obviously great freedom and informality about it. From this passage two great questions emerge":

(1)   "Clearly the early church had no professional ministry......."

(2)   "There was obviously flexibility about the order of service in the early church......"

(www.studylight.org/com/dsb, *William Barclay's Daily Study Bible, 1Corinthians 14*).

"Each one" can participate and contribute in this meeting (consider the limitation placed on women in verse 34). The meeting is open for a number of men to take part with a view to edification. It was a meeting superintended by the Holy Spirit. As Macdonald observes, "Paul gives tacit approval to this "open meeting" where there was liberty for the Spirit of God to speak through different brothers" (William MacDonald, *Believer's Bible Commentary*, 1801). Almost all reputed New Testament scholars, irrespective of church affiliation, have admitted that this is the way the early church met.

Following the pattern found in the New Testament meeting of the Church, the assemblies follow a simple service, without any settled format or order of service. Most of the features found in the order of service in many Christian churches today are a carryover from the Old Testament worship. Several denominational churches also have become dissatisfied with the traditional, rigid, liturgical, clergy-dominated (controlled) set order of worship service, and have switched to more spontaneous types of worship. The Charismatic movement has popularized free worship (sometime called "Prophetic Worship") around the world. Among Roman Catholics and in most denominations today, there are separatist or splinter groups who gather together to enjoy the blessings and benefits of spontaneous prayer, singing and worship.

A Review & Reflection of Our "Open Meetings"

As a company of God's people, we are privileged and blessed to follow the simplicity of the New Testament in our gatherings. How we enjoy the sweetness of such a meeting! But we must also bear in mind that we do not have **all the details** in the New Testament of the early Christian worship. We have only a glimpse of some essential elements from 1 Cor.11 and 14. I believe the most important things about the meeting of the church are revealed to us, and we should not be unnecessarily bogged down by other details or non-essentials.

But we have to search ourselves and see whether we advocate an 'order of service' of our own. Are we not easily disturbed if anything changes from it? Some local assemblies slavishly hold on to the idea that the way they conduct their worship meeting is the *real* biblical pattern and the *only* way to worship the Lord, and they look down upon all others who differ from them. According to our own preferences, we spell out *what* can be done and should be done (what is permissible) and *what* cannot be done and *when* it can be done or *when* it cannot be done. When we do this, are we not imposing another humanly devised system? This may not be true about every assembly, but it may be true of most. There is need for more flexibility and graciousness in this matter. If the meeting is to be Spirit-led, then it is not to be bound by our preferences, traditions or settled order of service.

We also need to remember that the meeting of the church found in 1 Cor.14 was *not* exclusively a "worship meeting." It was also a meeting for the Spirit-led exercise of spiritual gifts. That means we need to have some unstructured periods with a view to allow the Holy Spirit to spontaneously use some brethren to teach, preach, or to exhort the assembly through their spiritual gifts. During the "worship" meeting it is the practice of the assemblies (a good one) to be more focused on the Lord and what the emblems represent. But most assemblies do not have the time devoted to the free exercise of spiritual gifts for edification (as we find in 1

Cor.14:26). This aspect of the spontaneous exercise of spiritual gifts of the "meeting of the church" is really overlooked. We may need some radical changes to implement it in our meetings.

Since we place a very high value on the open meeting of the church on Sunday morning, we must also constantly evaluate the quality of such meetings, and see how we can maximize the blessings and benefits of this meeting as we come together as the priesthood of God. It places a great responsibility, especially on the men, to come prepared than to be laid back and passively watch the meeting (I remember a sister telling me once that "If you men allow us to audibly participate in the meeting, then we will show you what real worship is!").

Some new and young believers may not know the importance and the need for preparation and spirit-filled exercises in the meeting. This needs to be taught and reminded. The elders have a responsibility in this matter. This writer remembers his early days in the assembly and how godly elders imparted wise counsel, teaching and encouragement in relation to the Sunday meeting. This made a profound impact upon me in worship and participation in assembly gatherings. I have been in assemblies where these matters are never discussed, reminded or taught. It is taken for granted that everyone knows it. So they just continue with a routine, dry like a rock! We learn through instruction and example. Pastoral motivation is a vital part of leadership ministry.

Being led by the Spirit (the Holy Spirit is our worship leader) in the open meeting does not preclude individual preparation, and participation should be orderly, reverent and edifying (it is not "just sharing" something). Only what is edifying is to be permitted in the meeting ("Let all things be done for edification"). By the statement "each one has...." (1 Cor.14:26) Paul is not suggesting that every individual audibly participated in the meeting, but it only means *each one was free to participate* in the meeting (Paul himself spells out restriction in the number of participants in 14:29). All were free to be involved but with mutual consideration and with a view to edify others. Our freedom is to be exercised in love and with a sense of responsibility and accountability. The Lord never expects one person to dominate the meeting. Church is not about the individual, it is about the Body. We come to give and to receive. Paul also reminds, "Order in the church!"

Five kinds of participation are mentioned in **1Cor.14:26**. All of these items except *psalms* (singing or reading an Old Testament psalm) are **related to one's spiritual gifts** (*teaching, revelation, tongues, interpretation of tongues*). What conclusion can we draw with reference to the participatory role in the open meeting? When the church met, anyone was free to participate. Prayer, praise, singing, and reading of the Word all have its place. *But the overall* *emphasis falls on balanced, spirit-led and considerate participation on the part of members with the exercise of their speaking gifts to edify others.* The privilege of participation should not be abused or misused to the point of disorder.

Practical Points to Ponder

In an open worship pattern, we have to be very cautious about several practical matters. Otherwise, we may encounter more disadvantages with the "open" worship. Let us not jump to the conclusion that only those who audibly participated worshipped the Lord or they are the only "spiritual ones." It is desirable that more people participate audibly in an orderly manner. No one should be pressured to participate just to please others. When there is more time allowed for open worship in many places, things are done just to *fill* the silence and the time. Periods of silence are good as opportunities for individual silent worship and meditation. But silence also can be indicative of lack of spiritual urge and preparation (when there is a *long silence* usually one of the elders is compelled to finally break it!).In some assemblies "open worship time" is just an "open singing" time (In an assembly a visitor once asked me, "What will happen here if we remove all the hymnbooks?"). Some men who otherwise may not get the pulpit may be tempted to selfishly use the open time for "preaching", to make a display of their knowledge to others.

I believe some regulations and planning are helpful (without being dogmatic, I want to be realistic) in relation to the time, number of songs, other practical guidelines and suggestions that can be helpful to various activities in the meeting (to be graciously given and not legalistically imposed). There is also nothing essentially wrong in someone opening up with a welcome, a song, helpful guidelines and reminders for the meeting, and an appropriate meditation or exhortation to set the tone for the gathering. After a good Word from the Lord, more time can be set aside for praise and prayer, singing, reading and meditation; or even before the breaking of bread or close of the service, a word from the Word may be really refreshing by someone assigned to do it.

Those who can lead in singing may be asked to assist the congregation that it may result in good, vibrant, orderly singing to the glory of God. Some of us need to change the mindset that God places a premium on "dryness" which is a major complaint about the meeting in many assemblies. The men who audibly participate also may be reminded at times to be sensitive to the time, context, and the people around them.

These suggestions are not universally applicable to all assemblies. But wherever there is a need, we should be willing to make appropriate changes for the glory of God and the blessing of His people. Some of the regulators, controls, and planning we bring into the meeting of the church is no way hindering the leadership of the Spirit. It will actually make the "open meeting" more profitable and edifying, and honoring to the Lord. *Remember, Paul himself spelled out regulations for the open meeting! In most assemblies the elders regulate and plan at least some elements and logistics of the open meeting.* We use regulatory principles in all areas of our life though we totally trust the Lord and live under His Lordship. When we act responsibly to honor the Lord, we are glorifying Him. After all, we are commanded to love the Lord with all our heart, all our soul, all our mind, and with all our strength" (Mark 12:30).

In the early days of the Brethren movement, many people were impressed and attracted by the "breaking of bread" meeting of the Brethren. That still stands out as one of the most important distinctives of the Brethren. I had the privilege of meeting some believers (from non-Brethren backgrounds) who accepted the Lord as their Savior in the breaking of bread meeting of the assemblies. I was thrilled to hear their testimonies. Such is the power and blessing of remembrance and worship if we observe it as it should be observed. Those who have left the assemblies always say that they really miss the "breaking of bread".

At the same time, there is a general complaint from young and old alike that our meetings are becoming just a routine, dull, and dry.

If this is what many of us feel, what about "others" who may be attending our meetings? This is not something new. In 1983, Donald Norbie pointed out this problem in very strong language. It needs to be heeded again. He wrote:

"Some meetings have the gloom of a morgue rather than the joy of the Lord. Singing should be animated and happy. Some of the newer songs and choruses can be most worshipful as well as the older hymns......encourage the sharing of the Word. The hymn book is opened too often and the Bible too little. At some meeting the Bible may never be used. A hymn, a prayer, a hymn, a prayer......the Word ministered in freshness by the Holy Spirit will stir hearts as nothing else. Brethren need to be in the Word on Saturday night instead of in the TV tube. "They shall not appear before the Lord empty" (Deut.16:16) [*The early Church*, Christian Missions Press, 1983, 39].

We cannot just leave this matter at diagnosis, however, but prayerfully consider ways to reform the "open meetings." I believe it starts with good teaching, followed by discussions, prayer, reminders, creating more awareness, and above all, a willingness to CHANGE. I believe the leadership of every assembly has to play a decisive role in carrying out these action plans.

"And on the first day of the week, when we were gathered together to break bread...." (Acts 20: 7).

The Need for Broader Participation in the Remembrance Meeting

(The following brief article was prepared by this author and distributed in his home assembly to encourage the young people to actively participate in the open "worship meeting." Later this was published in an assembly magazine").

Our worship/Remembrance/Lord's Supper meeting is not led or controlled by a group of professional ministers. What a liberating truth! It is supremely important for us as New Testament priests to perform acts of worship as we gather together to remember the Lord. The men in the assembly have the privilege and opportunity to audibly participate in this priestly service of spiritual sacrifices (Heb.13:15; 1Peter 2:5). This is our birthright, a real practical demonstration of the great doctrine of the priesthood of believers.

But the truth of the matter is, only a very small number of men are willing to participate in the meeting from week to week, and often the same men every week! Most of the young people in the assembly are silent during this time, though they are active in other areas of service. This is a valid concern shared by the leadership of many assemblies. This widespread problem robs the assembly of fresh, vibrant, and inspiring worship.

Though brief meditations from the Word and announcing a hymn have all its place, **the most**

important thing is to praise and worship the Lord by pouring out our hearts before Him. A spontaneous outpouring of gratitude in worship is the most important element in worship. Even if we share a brief comment or thought from the Word appropriate to the occasion (which is well and good), let us make sure we conclude it with a word of prayer expressive of our worship. Though we are not guided by legalistic rules, **the most valuable way to contribute in the Lord's Supper is to simply offer a short prayer of praise, adoration and worship.** It adds vibrancy and life to our worship. This seems to be a lost art among God's people in many parts of the world.

Let me share a personal note here: My parents, early mentors and elders always encouraged and instructed the young men in our assembly to be **active first in the worship meeting.** Many in my generation can testify to the same approach. Meaningful and vibrant worship was a high priority and that was the first step young people were encouraged to take. A.P. Gibb's book, *Worship: The Christian's Highest Occupation* was the present given to me by my parents after my baptism. This was the sentiment shared by assembly believers world over. They wanted to make sure that the Lord's Supper meeting is always fresh, meaningful, enjoyable and inspiring.

Prior preparation will definitely help us in meaningful participation in the Lord's Supper. Let me quote A. P. Gibbs: "God's Word to Israel was: "None shall appear before me empty" (Exod.23:15). It is pathetic indeed, at a meeting convened particularly for worship, to see so many who apparently have neither taken the time nor made the effort to put anything in their basket of gratitude. The long periods of silence in many worship meetings are often, not the silences of worshipful adoration, but the silences of spiritual poverty."

Let us all commit ourselves to rediscover the power, grandeur and blessing of real worship. Remember, the Breaking of Bread Meeting is the most cherished distinctive of the Brethren Assemblies. Please prayerfully consider how you can personally contribute to the blessing of this most important of meetings. Make a new decision in your life to be a diligent worshipper more than anything else.

(Three years ago Bro. Mike Stephenson wrote a book titled, *New Testament Priests, Speak Up* {Published by ECS Publications}. This is a very challenging book addressing the need for more participation in the Lord's Supper. He observes some of the deficiencies in our worship meeting and points out ways to remedy it. He also gives simple and practical guidelines to encourage and equip the men for more meaningful participation. A MUST read).

12

Antioch Model of Missions

*"Set apart for Me, Barnabas and Saul for the work
to which I have called them" (Acts 13:2)*

The history of missions in the book of Acts
provides the basic principles and guidelines for
missions today. The church at Antioch (Acts 13) is
the biblical model for missions. The assemblies have
strived to follow this model. In the New Testament,
missions were carried out by the local churches.
Missionaries were sent out from churches and not
from mission boards or para-church organizations.
Though there is a total departure from the biblical
model of missions today, the Brethren assemblies
are still committed to the New Testament pattern
on missions. This was exemplified from the very
early days of the Brethren movement through great
heroes of faith like George Muller and Anthony
Norris Groves, who is known as the "Father of Faith
Missions."

What is the Antioch model of missions? Several characteristics of the Antioch model of missions are found in Acts 13:1-4.

1. The Antioch church had a deep burden for evangelization. They came together for fasting and prayer.
2. The leadership of the assembly consisted of prophets and teachers. It was a well- taught assembly. The mission of the church at Antioch was born out of fasting, prayer, worship, and Word.
3. The call to missionary service came to those who were already serving the Lord in the church. They were not novices in the work of the Lord. The assembly was energized, and equipped by the Holy Spirit for enlarged missionary activities. The Holy Spirit directed that Barnabas and Saul be set apart for a special ministry.
4. The call was from God, made known by the Holy Spirit to the church.
5. The call was recognized and confirmed by the local church. They knew very how to discern the will and mind of God.
6. The church expressed their whole-hearted support and identification with the missionaries. "They laid their hands on them" as an expression of fellowship, identification, and unity with them in the work to which the Holy Spirit had called them. This was an act of commendation and commission for a special service with the full blessing and support of the church.

7. It was after the church had fasted and prayed that they sent Barnabas and Saul. "They sent them away" literally means, "they let them go." They were *released* to the work for which the Lord had called them. Acts 13:4 states, "they being sent forth by the Holy Spirit." The real commissioning was by God, not man.

8. It was from Antioch that they had been commended to the grace of God (Acts 14:26; 15:40). Thus, there was a sense of partnership between the local church and the missionaries. There was a ready recognition that the work in which they were engaged was one in which the church collectively shared. It was thus regarded as an extension or overflow of the church's ministry.

9. While the most intimate fellowship existed between the missionaries and the local church, they were not under their control, and had full liberty to engage in the work to which the Lord had called them.

10. The missionaries looked to God for direction and guidance in their service. In Acts 16:6-10 we see Paul, Silas, and Luke most uncertain about their future course. But they looked to God alone and He directed their path to the right place. Consultation, counsel, and mutual understanding between the commending assembly and the missionaries are always desirable and good. It fosters a sense of accountability and responsibility. But the final

decision should be between the missionary and His Lord.

11. It is surprising that the one thing that is not mentioned in the mission passages in Acts is *finance*. How vastly different from some of the modern practices where matters of money is the first and foremost (sometimes the only thing) emphasized in relation to missions. The missionaries totally depended on the Lord for the supply of their temporal needs. Local churches ministered to their needs (Phil.4:15-18; 1:5; 2 Cor.11:8). Paul sets for the principle in 1 Cor.9:14 that "those who preach the gospel should receive their living from the gospel."

Our Lord is "the Lord of the harvest." He is totally in charge of missions. He cares for and takes interest in all those who are faithfully serving Him in the field. Standing on these convictions, the assemblies do not encourage solicitation of funds or publicity with a motive of raising finances. At the same time, we should not forget our responsibility in financially supporting those who are serving the Lord. The Lord uses His people as instruments in supplying His servant's needs.

The assemblies do not follow any legalistic rules concerning Christian giving. Giving is an act of worship and the Scripture exhorts us to give regularly, cheerfully, systematically, freely, liberally and proportionately (2 Cor.8-9; 1 Cor.16:12). No financial support is taken from the unsaved. More planned, strategic, and considerate support of missionaries is to be encouraged in assemblies (see chapter 8 for more discussion on the **support** of those who serve the Lord full-time).

There are a number of missions and missionaries in the active service of the Lord around the globe in a commendable way that may have different convictions and practices in relation to their work. We should not be judgmental of them though they may differ with us in some of their methodologies. They stand or fall to their master. One of the great needs in several mission fields around the world is more cooperation and united gospel efforts between missionaries, wherever and whenever that is possible. We should be open to such opportunities for the furtherance of the Gospel. Our idea of biblical "separation" should not lead us to an "isolationist" mentality (Biblical *separation* is sometimes misinterpreted as *isolation* from other Christians).

We have a great responsibility to carry on the mission of God with passion and vision. Methods, models, programs, and strategies are all necessary for effectively carrying out missions. Certain efforts such as evangelism seminars, training in missions and missionary methods, systematic teaching on the biblical theology of missions, and more awareness about mission fields, are currently being done in some assemblies. We need to continue such activities on a regular basis. In many mission fields in the past, there was a neglect of training centers and Bible schools to teach and train local believers and leaders. This has adversely affected the growth of local assemblies. That situation has considerably changed today with very positive results in the mission fields.

Supernatural Power

Methods, models, or marketing strategies are not the vital issues in missions. These elements are not the first or most crucial issues in prompting success and blessing in missions. The critical issue is the supernatural empowering of the church. The assemblies have always believed and promoted it. This is the path for our young zealous missionaries of the future. "You shall receive power when the Holy Spirit has come upon you; and you shall be My witnesses both in Jerusalem, and in all Judea and Samaria, and even to the remotest part of the earth (Acts 1:8). Many zealous and enthusiastic missionaries today try to do missions by ignoring the biblical theology of missions. The attempt to do "missions" through a certain *method* is an attempt to do supernatural work through natural power. Divine power (Acts 1:8) and our adherence to the divine pattern unfolded in the Word (Acts 13) will produce missions in the real biblical sense. This is the Antioch model. **The Antioch model creates an Antioch effect.**

"And from there they sailed to Antioch from which they had been commended to the grace of God for the work that they had accomplished" (Acts 14:26).

13
The Practice of Head Covering

"Therefore the woman ought to have a symbol of
authority on her head because of the angels"
(1 Cor.11:10)

The question of women's place in the church is a much debated issue today. What the Bible does say about this matter is drowned out by what culture tells us. Though there is a rejection of the biblical teaching on the role of women in church and ministry in most evangelical circles, generally speaking, the assemblies still follow the plain teaching of scripture in this matter. But this is undergoing radical change even among some assemblies. They are also tempted and pressured by "cultural churchianity" to abandon biblical guidelines on women's role in the church.

In obedience to the instruction laid down in Scripture (1 Cor.14:34-35; 1 Tim.2:11-12; 1Tim.2:8; Tit.2:3-5), women do not speak publicly in the gathering of the church and do not take leadership positions, or exercise authority over men. We believe this is a valid transcultural precept, based on the Scriptural principle of headship. However, this principle does not infer that women do not have equal standing before God or that their role in church life is less valuable than men. In the oneness

144

of the body of Christ (the redemption order) there is neither male nor female – "all one in Christ Jesus" (Gal.3:28). Women are encouraged to have wide sphere of ministries, for which they are particularly suited. This is the position the assemblies hold on to in relation to the ministry of women in the church.

If an assembly is convinced that there are particular areas of ministry/ service where women may take part, and if the Bible is silent on theses specific areas, without contradicting the clear biblical principles, the elders of those assemblies may responsibly set the guidelines for them to follow.

The Practice of Head Covering Today

Head covering has become a very controversial subject. Most churches do not even want to hear about it. It is a symbol in decline and in rejection. The Brethren assemblies teach and practice head covering for women in the church meeting. We believe that the Christian doctrine of order in creation, involving subordination and headship, requires the Christian practice of manifesting that order in public worship by the veiling of women (head covering). Lot of changes have happened in recent years and many assemblies have abandoned this practice, and others have made it an optional issue, without teaching it or attaching any significance to it. But this has been one of the distinctives of the assemblies all over the world. We may find a very small segment in other conservative-evangelical churches in the West that may practice it today. In Asian and African churches, most women follow this practice (the exception may be only to westernized Christians in these countries). In some countries, head covering is a part of the women's dress, and hence there is no controversy over it in relation to church gathering.

It is a fact that head covering was practiced in many churches until the early 70's. But the "Women's Liberation" movement, both in its liberal and evangelical versions, started influencing the Western churches, and then slowly spread to other parts of the world. The feminist ideologies have influenced churches and Christian academic institutions. These ideologies also have adversely affected the family structure and have fueled a cultural revolt against the authority of the husband over the wife. As a result, evangelical churches began to give an increased public role to women beyond the Scriptural guidelines. Many evangelical theologians, Bible colleges and seminaries "revised" their doctrine of the role of women in the Church. Some of them were "pressured" to do it for popularity and academic prestige. Along with this "revolution", head covering became a very contentious issue, and was abandoned by many (including some assemblies). I believe, the abandonment of head covering is tied to the rejection of biblical roles of men and women.

It seems that 1 Cor.11:16 was prophetic as though Paul knew that the head covering doctrine will become very controversial and many will be contentious about it – "But if one is inclined to be contentious….."

What does the Bible specifically teach about head covering? Is this a cultural issue (related to the particular situation in Corinth) and not applicable to us today, as most Bible scholars interpret it? Is this really important as Paul mentions it only once in his letters? How far is this applicable to us today? These are really important and relevant questions that need to be addressed in the assemblies, especially for the sake of the young generation and new believers. In many assemblies, although there is a strict adherence to the practice of head covering, there is often a lack of clear teaching on this subject.

We assume that believers know the Scriptural reasons for the head covering and it is seldom taught or discussed today. A vast majority of sisters who cover their head do not know why they do so. This is equally true of brothers, as they also do not know why they keep their heads uncovered in the church. Since planned, systematic, consecutive, need-oriented pulpit teaching by gifted men is missing in most assemblies (as pointed out in the previous chapters), believers do not get an opportunity to study and evaluate matters of the faith. It is not surprising that here are numerous lingering questions in the minds of our sisters in many assemblies in relation to head covering, though they have practiced it for years. This is the reason this subject is dealt with in this book in some detail, though not exhaustively.

(For an in-depth study of the head covering, I recommend the book by Warren Henderson, *Glories Seen & Unseen*, Livingstone Bookshop Limited, Hong Kong, 2003. Also available at Gospel Folio Press, Canada. The website www.headcoveringmovement.com provides numerous resources for historical, theological, and exegetical defense of the doctrine and practice of head covering).

Head Covering: A Symbolic Truth

A symbol is an act or object that teaches a spiritual truth. It represents or stands for something else. Head covering is symbolic and there is meaning behind the covered head of a woman in the context of the church ("symbol of authority" in 1 Cor.11:10 is one word in Greek and simply mean "power" or "authority." "Symbol" (as in NASB) is implied because of the obvious reference to head covering in the context). Besides Head Covering, **two other prominent symbols also are mentioned in 1 Cor.11-**

the *bread* and the *wine*. The first part of 1 Cor.11 explains the meaning of the *symbolic head covering* for women and the second part of the chapter explains the meaning of the *symbolic bread and cup* in the Lord's Supper.

Baptism is another important symbol in the Christian faith. Rom.6 and other passages explain the meaning of this symbol. The Book of Revelation is full of symbols. But the symbols are there to illuminate the truth. *No one can say that symbols have no significance in the Bible. They are really important. Spiritual significance is attached to these symbols.* Would we say that Baptism and the Lord's Supper are unimportant, because they are only symbols? How can anyone pick and choose between these symbols and say that one is important and the other is not? These symbols represent important spiritual truths. Symbols in Christian faith are not for symbol's sake, but to represent the reality and substance behind it; hence it is important and not to be discarded.

It's Importance

If God has given us a command to obey, even if it is commanded only once, it is important. The importance of a command is determined by the person giving the command. Moreover, in 1 Cor.11:16, Paul says that there is no practice of women worshipping without head covering in the

149

churches of God (the "practice" or "custom" here refers to women appearing uncovered and not the practice of being contentious). This custom goes beyond Corinth, and Christians elsewhere followed it (contentiousness is an *attitude* or temper, not a *custom*). A departure and a disorder in this matter is only found in Corinth. "But if one is inclined to be contentious, we have no other practice, nor have the churches of God." In using "we" he means other apostles. His teaching is of apostolic authority and not just a pious advice. **Head covering was a uniform practice in the apostolic churches**. Paul taught all the churches this custom and he expected them to follow it.

Paul regarded the matter of head covering as important and worth deciding, and does not simply brush it as trivial. What the apostle is teaching is a part of the apostolic "traditions" (11: 2, not "ordinances" as in KJV) – the package of *doctrine* he was passing on to the church. In other words, his first appeal is to the apostolic Word. Further, he wants them to "understand" the truths which he is writing (11:3), and then he appeals to the universal practice in the apostolic churches (11:16). The apostolic authority of his instructions is well-established. That is why He also wanted the Corinthian Christians to abide by it. They should not question the accepted practice of all God's people elsewhere. Paul was teaching them practices important to the church. Let no one dare to treat it today as *unimportant*.

In 1 Cor.14 (in the context of women's silence in the church), Paul also insists that what he teaches as an apostle is the truth of God, and it was not optional. One who does not respect and accept Paul's words should not have his own words respected or accepted (1 Cor.14:37-38).

The Cultural Argument

Contrary to popular opinion today, there is *absolutely nothing* in Paul's reasons for head covering, based upon custom or culture. Paul does not appeal to any social custom of his day. No cultural information is required to interpret this passage. Paul did not make any reference to culture here. Theologians and commentators are the ones forcing the cultural argument on Paul. One will search in vain to find a cultural reference unless it is forced upon the text. Women are not commanded to wear a veil because of some cultural issues (e.g. to distinguish them from temple prostitutes in Corinth. The numerous cultural theories vary and cannot be unequivocally asserted).

The fallacy of the cultural argument has been forcefully brought out by the Reformed theologian R. C. Sproul when he states:

"Some very subtle means of relativizing the text occur when we read into the text cultural considerations that ought not to be there. For example, with respect to the hair covering issue in Corinth, numerous commentators on the Epistle point out that the local sign of the prostitute in Corinth was the uncovered head. Therefore, the argument runs, the reason why Paul wanted women to cover their heads was to avoid a scandalous appearance of Christian women in the external guise of prostitutes.

What is wrong with this kind of speculation? The basic problem here is that our reconstructed knowledge of first century Corinth has led us to supply Paul with a rationale that is foreign to the one he gives himself. In a word, we are not only putting words into the apostle's mouth, but we are ignoring words that are there. If Paul merely told women in Corinth to cover their heads and gave no rationale for such instruction, we will be strongly inclined to supply it via our cultural knowledge. In this case, however, Paul provides a rationale which is based on an appeal to creation not to the custom of Corinthian harlots. We must be careful not to let our zeal for knowledge of the culture obscure what is actually said. To subordinate Paul's stated reason to our speculatively conceived reason is to slander the apostle and turn exegesis into eisegesis.

The creation ordinances are indicators of the transcultural principle. If any biblical principles transcend local customary limits, they are the appeals drawn from creation" (R. C. Sproul, *Knowing Scripture*, Inter-Varsity Press, 1977, 110).

In the same chapter of the book (Chapter 5, Culture & the Bible) Sproul points out some valid obstacles in Bible interpretation which throws more light on our subject. This is what he says:

"It often becomes difficult for me to hear and understand what the Bible is saying because I bring to it a host of extra-biblical assumptions. This is probably the biggest problem of "cultural conditioning" we face.....I am convinced that the problem of the influence of the twentieth- century secular mindset is a far more formidable obstacle to accurate biblical interpretation than is the problem of the conditioning of the ancient culture" (*Knowing Scripture*, 104-105).

Cultural situations throw light upon certain biblical passages and have a bearing on interpretation. But the guiding principle is that we have to investigate the cultural reason if no theological rationale is given by the writer. Cultural reason should not be used to undermine what the text clearly teaches. Also, the teaching given in the overall context is crucial in understanding the meaning of a given passage. This is a determining factor in deciding whether some practices are culture bound or transcultural. In the case of head covering, Paul's arguments are unambiguously based on theological considerations drawn from the creation narratives and the doctrine of headship. The whole context is doctrinally oriented in correcting some disorders in the Corinthian assembly. Moreover, the practice of head covering is also *commanded* and not just mentioned in passing as a culturally conditioned practice.

The practice of head covering was not restricted to Corinth. It was a custom in all the apostolic churches of that time (1 Cor.11:16) and not something conditioned by a particular cultural situation in a geographical area. Paul did not say anything about culture in relation to the head covering. It is the commentators and theologians who are saying it. S. Lewis Johnson said it well:

"Every reason that Paul gives for the head covering is not cultural and yet evangelicals frequently say, 'oh well, that's a cultural thing; we don't have to pay attention to it.' The reasons are not cultural. Creation. Woman's hair itself. Nature itself. Angelic beings are looking down upon us. Those are not cultural reasons" (sljinstitute.net/pauls epistles/1 Corinthians).

Is The Hair Itself the Head Covering?

Some authors have maintained that when Paul says, "For her hair is given to her for a covering" (1 Cor.11:15), he is saying that the hair itself is the head covering. This has become a very popular interpretation. But this cannot be the meaning of Paul's statement for several reasons:

1. After establishing the need for head covering in the first 14 verses, is Paul contradicting himself in v.15? Is he simply saying that *a woman should have long hair and that's all he is teaching*. He could have stated that in one simple sentence!

2. The Greek word for covering in v.15 (*peribolaion*) means a "mantle," (Heb.1:12) "a covering around," " a wrap" and is different from Paul's earlier usage for "covering" or "uncovering" in verses 4-7 (*katakalupto*) which means to "veil" or "to cover down upon." This word is not used elsewhere in the New Testament to refer to hair. One is a reference to a woman's natural covering - nature has endowed her with long hair - the other to a physical/external/symbolic covering; a material covering. It seems that the difference in words is intentional. "Unless one sees two coverings are mentioned in this chapter, the passage becomes hopelessly confusing" (William MacDonald, *Believer's Bible Commentary*, 1786).

3. If the hair is the covering intended by Paul, how will we explain the act of *covering* or *uncovering* (it makes sense only if it refers to a detachable object) mentioned in verses 5-6? Paul is talking about what a woman wears on her head at specific times (when engaged in acts of worship), and not always. So he is NOT talking about the hair but a removable object.

4. If a woman's hair was given instead of a physical covering, then Paul is teaching that women should pray with long hair, and not short hair which makes no sense.

5. If we apply this interpretation, and substitute "hair" for "covering" throughout this passage, see whether it makes any sense. The whole argument becomes ridiculous and nonsensical. "For a woman does not *cover* her head, let her also have hair cut off" means according to this interpretation, if a woman does not have her *hair* on, then she might just as well be shorn!! If she does not have hair on, how can she be shorn? In the same way, every man who prays or prophesies (11:4, 7) has to have his head shaved?

6. A woman's hair is given to her "for" a covering does **not mean** "in place of" a covering (the idea of substitution does not make any sense as shown above), but rather, "over against" and "corresponds to," to match the covering which she is required to wear in the public assembly.

7. Long hair serves as a natural covering to *all* women – believers and unbelievers. How then can the submission of a godly woman be evidenced by being just like every other woman?

To suggest that the hair replaces the head covering is to confuse the meaning of the passage and to ignore the truth Paul was teaching (the NIV footnote on 1 Cor.11:4-7 supporting this view is not an alternate translation, or plausible rendering, but a misleading *interpretation*, totally biased and indefensible).

Long hair is the woman's covering in the natural realm and the symbolic head covering in the spiritual realm. Since she has a covering in the physical realm, she should also have a covering in the spiritual realm. One is a permanent covering, the other a temporary covering.

The "long hair view" is a new and strange interpretation. It is totally different from how the church has understood this passage for nineteen hundred years. Several notable church fathers believed that Paul commanded a literal fabric covering or a veil. Until the twentieth century the practice of head covering was upheld by most Christians. "I do know this, that until fifty years ago, every woman in every church covered her head.....What has happened in the last fifty years? We've had a feminist movement" (R.C. Sproul). How true!

A woman's natural covering of glory (her personal glory) must be "covered" in the gathering of the church so that only God's glory may be seen. The fact that nature thus covers the woman's head with long hair is a guide for her to the spiritual truth of the head covering which she is required to wear in the Assembly of God. The intent of the head covering is not for fashion (one wonders whether the modern Western hat – so decorative, attractive, obstructive, and even distractive, can be a suitable symbol as Paul intended)!

Paul's Reasons for the Head Covering

Paul gives three basic reasons (theological) and two supportive reasons (practical) for head covering.
1.   **The divine order of headship - God, Christ, man, woman (1 Cor.11:3).**
2.   **The order in creation (11:7-9).**
3.   **The presence of angels in the meeting (11:10).**
4.   **Nature: Woman's long hair as a natural/personal covering (11:15).**
5.   **Universal church practice (11:16).**

Paul starts with **the theology of headship** in 1 Cor.11:3. Three heads are mentioned:
1.   God is the head of Christ.
2.   Christ is the head of the man.
3.   Man is the head of the woman.
   • Headship exists even within Godhead.

158

- "Woman" is the only one not called a "head".

Headship has the idea of leadership and authority. God the Son is not in any way inferior to God the Father. Divine order is in view here where there is willing subordination (only in a functional sense), and no inferiority is implied. There is equality in being, but difference in roles. The headship-subordination order is not established to enforce superiority or inferiority in relationships. Rather it is meant to promote peace and harmony in relationships. This divine ordering is integral to God's creation, government, church, and the family. Without structures of headship all of these institutions would collapse into chaos. "Subordination does not necessarily involve inequality. Headship is not the same as lordship" (S. Lewis Johnson, 1 Corinthians, *The Wycliffe Bible Commentary*, Moody Press, 1990, 1247).

Next Paul brings in **the order in creation (1 Cor.11:7-9)**. The *headship* of the man and the *subordination* of the woman are now seen in the light of the creation order.
- Adam was created first and directly, woman was created *from* man (Adam came in by *creation*, and Eve by *formation*).
- Woman *for* the man – to complement and support him, to be his companion.
- Man is the image and glory of God.

- Woman is the glory of the man.

Paul calls our attention here to the divine design in creation, reminding us of headship and subordination in man –woman relationships. It is **ONLY** functional subordination and not ontological inferiority. The headship-submission relationship is proved from the order of the Godhead (theological hierarchy) and the order in creation. After showing the distinctions between the sexes, in **verses 11-12** Paul asserts their interdependence. Husbands and wives have equal worth before God. God originates both of them, and both are subordinate to God.

Male-female distinctions, their mutual interdependence, headship -submission principle are not culturally conditioned, but it is a permanent doctrine binding on us, divinely ordained and ordered. "All things originate from God" (11:12). So the foundational reason for head covering is the created order. Headship and authority is God's original intent in creation even before sin entered the world. It is not a post-Fall disaster.

Note the three glories:

1. Man is the glory of God (11:7).
2. Woman is the glory of the man (11:7).
3. Woman's long hair her personal glory, naturally given to her (11:15).

The Meaning of Head Covering

On the basis of the Scriptural truths explained above, the meaning of head covering may be summarized in this way:

1. A man should not cover his head, because he is the image and glory of God. *God's glory should not be covered.*

2. Since the woman is the glory of man, *the glory of man must be covered* in the church through the head covering of woman. When she covers her head she is testifying to this truth.

3. *The glory of the woman also must be covered.* A woman's long hair, which is her personal and natural glory (1 Cor.11: 15), must be covered in the church, just like the glory of man is covered. In the church the woman places a covering on her head, thus not only veiling man's glory which she represents, but her own personal glory, her long hair. If she refuses to be covered, let her also have her hair cut off (her personal and natural glory) which is totally disgraceful to her (11:6).

4. Man represents the glory of God and therefore, he wears no covering. The woman representing man's glory is covered. Her natural and personal glory also is covered.

5. *Only God's glory is to be seen in the church.* The uncovered head of man teaches that God's glory alone is to be seen; it should not be veiled. The

woman with covered head, not only veils her own glory, but also man's glory.

6. It also symbolizes her subordination to the man and her willingness to be submissive to man's authority. She accepts her God-appointed role in the order of headship and preserves the order of creation. Head covering thus becomes a woman's witness to *her exalted view of the principle of submission*.

7. Only the glory of God is seen in the church. An *exalted view of the glory of God in the church* is the ultimate truth that is proclaimed in this doctrine. All glory goes to God alone, and not to anyone else. "To Him be the glory in the church and in Christ Jesus to all generations forever and ever. Amen" (Eph.3:21).

"Because of the Angels"

Yet another reason for the woman's head covering is based upon the presence of angels in the gatherings of the church. The proponents of the cultural and social arguments have a real problem here. "Therefore the woman ought to have a *symbol* of authority on her head because of the angels" (1 Cor.11:10). A specific reason is stated which can never be stretched to fit into the mold of cultural argument. Angels are a reason why we obey this command – "because of the angels." Women in the church cover their heads for the sake of angels. This practice is not just a witness to people, but to a completely different group of beings. They are not affected by culture or social custom. Head covering is based on timeless and transcultural truths.

The head covering symbolizes a woman's willingness to accept God's created order; to be submissive to man's headship (authority and leadership). Thus, she is submissive before God. The angels pay attention to the gatherings of the church. They are learning the manifold wisdom of God in the church (Eph.3:10; 1 Pet.1:12). What God is doing on earth is a part of His plan to display His glory to the angelic beings. The angels rejoiced watching God make the world (Job 38:4-7). They are aware of the created order. A woman participating in the church meetings without head covering is disrespecting the wisdom of God manifested through the church. The angels respect the will of God and carry out the will of God. They too cover themselves in the holy presence of God (Isa.6:2).

Good angels are an example of subordination, while the fallen angels fell because they were not submissive to God's authority. Women in the assembly by covering their heads are testifying even to angels, the truth of submission. We have to show them that we have only God's glory manifested in the church. Angels rejoice to see submission and order at work in the church. The angels are a silent cosmic audience in the church gathering. They were present at creation when headship was established (Job 38:7). Angels are presently engaged in ministering to saints (Heb.1:14).

"Therefore the woman ought to have......." Or "for this reason" (1 Cor.11:10 NKJV). The reason is theological and it is given in the text. It is found in exegesis, not in cultural analysis.

Universal Church Practice

Paul's final argument for head covering came from the universal church practice. This goes beyond Corinth and is the practice of all churches. The apostolic churches have no practice of women worshipping without head covering. His teachings in 1 Cor.11:2-16 go far beyond the cultural conditions affecting the Corinthian church (another blow to the cultural argument). The head covering in worship was universally the practice of Christian women until the twentieth century. Do we have to assume that some scholars suddenly found out some new truth to which the saints for thousand years were totally blind?

Head covering was the normal custom in the churches established on apostolic teaching and authority and should be maintained ("We" in this verse is the apostolic "we)." If one is inclined to be contentious, we have no other practice, nor have the churches of God" (1 Cor.11:16). The apostles and the apostolic churches were firmly committed to the practice of head covering. The uniformity of this practice was established in other assemblies also. "Authority is the only end of controversy with such disturbers of peace" (Charles Hodge).

To further establish his arguments and the authority of his teaching, Paul appealed to the fact that he taught the commandments of the Lord. "If anyone thinks he is a prophet or spiritual, let him recognize that the things which I write to you are the Lord's commandment" (1 Cor.14:37). His teachings were not opinions or options. God Himself is the ultimate source of his authority.

The five reasons of head covering as summarized by Warren Henderson in the last chapter of his book (Chapter 14,117-120) *Glories Seen & Unseen* can be really helpful to the readers:
1. To show agreement with divine order and headship.
2. To ensure God's glory is seen and competing glories are concealed.
3. The angels are watching and learning about submission and order.
4. Nature itself teaches the significance of the glories.
5. The Corinthian Church was unusual from other church gatherings.

It is really surprising that there is a general trend in Christianity to belittle or downplay the significance of the three major symbols – baptism,

Lord's Supper, and head covering. The doctrine of head covering is a glorious subject. It reminds us that our God is a God of distinctions. We are obliged to maintain the divinely prescribed distinctions. To present this doctrine, Paul knits together a wealth of teaching in a masterly way. We can see a perfect blending of Theology Proper, Christology, Anthropology, Ecclesiology, and gender theology in 1 Corinthians 11. It is unfortunate that most of Christendom today treat the teaching on head covering as trivial, and irrelevant. They fail to see the superb theology on which it rests, and the dignified position to which it elevates man and woman in the plan and purpose of God.

Dear sisters in Christ, in accepting the God-ordained place of submission to the headship of the man, and demonstrating it through the symbolic head covering, you are emulating the Son of God in His submission to the Father's will. Ultimately, you are glorifying God through your simple obedience in this matter. Remember, the devil is always against God's preeminence and glory, and our total submission to Him (he rebelled against it from the very beginning). "Satan persistently opposes the matter of head covering. It really puts him to shame" (Watchman Nee). Moreover, you are witnessing to the angelic observers that the divine order of headship which had been violated by the rebellion of Lucifer and the disobedience of Adam and Eve, has been restored in the redemption order inaugurated by the Son of God, our Lord and Savior. What a glorious truth to rejoice and to celebrate!

"Remember He did not entrust the visual beauty of the local assembly unto the brothers, but to the sisters. Sisters, you're on display for the entire universe to see. The angels are watching you. Will you be a glory seen or unseen?" (Warren Henderson, *Glories Seen & Unseen*, 120).

Anyone looking at 1 Cor.11:2-16 may recognize some of the interpretive problems confronting the expositor. But to treat this passage as unimportant, trivial and irrelevant is to rebel against God. During the majority of the church age, women covered their heads in the church. Women wearing hats to church was a common sight in the Western world until 1960's or early 70's. Then it was abandoned gradually over a period of time. Eventually, liberal trends and the influence of women's liberation movement brought many changes in dress, moral standards and biblical doctrines. This ultimately resulted in the abandonment of the symbol of God's order in the church. Unfortunately, even many evangelical scholars and theologians also yielded to the pressure of these "liberation" trends.

Some would even consider "Head covering" even as a humiliating practice. No doubt, it is the most *inconvenient* doctrine in this day and age, and hence the reluctance to follow it. Any teaching on headship, authority, submission and head covering go against the whims of our contemporary culture. It will be equated with *inequality*. None of these truths is politically correct! The world scoffs at any teaching that has the biblical idea of *submission* of women. Too many Christians (including evangelicals) are influenced in their thinking and actions by the world's standards. The world may accommodate *Cultural Christianity* (Churchianity?), but it will not tolerate *Biblical Christianity*. As the world tempts us to draw glory to ourselves, and to rebel against God, may we prove through our obedience even to the simple command of head covering that we long to live for the glory of God in total submission to His Lordship.

The Trend toward the "Meaningful Symbol View"

We acknowledge the fact that there are several respected evangelical bible scholars who seriously take the teaching on headship and head covering, though they do not support the view that literal head covering is applicable today. They also take into serious consideration the binding character of Paul's teaching and do not want to trivialize it in any way. According to this view, today's cultural setting is *different*, but the principles in 1 Cor.11 are *transferable* and to be followed by Christian women. The biblical symbol of head covering needs some sort of *corresponding symbol* today. This view is becoming popular in some conservative evangelical circles and some assemblies also lean more towards it.

But this view creates more problem than it solves. *What* corresponding symbols should we use today? Some would suggest wedding ring, modest dress, the way a woman talk about her husband, taking her husband's family name, and male leadership in the church and so on. Can we do real justice to the teaching of this passage by these alternate symbols of our own creation? Who will and how will we decide on a suitable alternative to the wearing of head coverings? Which symbols today represent headship and authority meaningfully? Are they all not relative to its meaning and significance? **Which symbol can communicate the intended meaning any more clearly than head covering**? Does the matter have to be decided by our whims and fancies? In this approach, the whole issue has to be decided purely on cultural and personal preferences, without any real objective control. It ends up in too much talk about the "principle" without the "practice."

Our approach to the doctrine and practice of head covering should not be a modern emulation of the days of judges, when "everyone did what was right in his own eyes." This is not a matter that is left to individual and cultural preferences. Do we have to accommodate the changing cultural views to

practice this doctrine? "This picture of His rule must not be seized by believers into their own hands to shape it according to their own pleasure. Ahaz incurred the wrath of God by changing the shape of the altar to conform it to Assyrian demands (2 Kings 16:10-11). Of course, the appearance of the headdress will change, just as the practice of the Lord's Supper may vary from culture to culture, but the symbol must be present or the reality and its truth may be lost" (Bruce K. Waltke,
1 Corinthians 11:2-16: An Interpretation, Bibliotheca Sacra 135, Dallas Theological Seminary Publication, January –March, 1978, 57).

It is inconceivable to this writer that the Spirit of God wants us to really struggle and wrestle on this doctrine before we can decide on an appropriate symbol for today, instead of the head covering. In that case, do we also have to reconsider other symbols of faith so that it may make more sense in the contemporary culture? The fact is we will never be able to decide. We don't have to decide, since it is already decided by our Creator-Redeemer God in His holy Word. Let us just obey it.

As we believe the doctrine of head covering and practice it, we must always bear in mind its true value and significance. William MacDonald calls our attention to this sublime truth when he writes:

"We might pause here to state that the head-covering is simply an outward sign and it is of value only when it is the outward sign of an inward grace. In other words, a woman might have a covering on her head and yet not truly be submissive to her husband. In such a case, to wear a head-covering would be of no value at all. The most important thing is to be sure that the heart is truly subordinate; then a covering on a woman's head becomes truly meaningful" (*Believer's Bible Commentary*, 1786).

Some Frequently Asked Questions on Head Covering

1. What should be our attitude to Christian women who are reluctant to wear a head covering?

A Christian woman should wear a head covering willingly and voluntarily out of conviction, and not under compulsion. This is not something that should be forced upon someone against her wish. Submission of the will is required in this matter, not just the obedience of the body. This is equally true of other aspects of Christian activities like baptism, Lord's Supper, prayer, Christian giving, fasting, witnessing, evangelism etc. We should not give the impression that wearing a head covering is a mark of spirituality or godly superiority; rather, we should be gracious in teaching them with patience and allowing the time for the Holy Spirit to work in their hearts so as to convict them. How much time (weeks or months) should be allowed is a matter of discretion by the elders of the local assembly.

Some of them do not wear it, because they never have been taught about it, or never thought about it as something important. Some may not do it because they are not still convinced that the Scriptures require them to do so. We must be sensitive to the fact that every woman coming through the doors of our assembly may not be from an "assembly background" or from churches that are committed to the practice of head covering. This may be a new truth to them. So we have to be gracious as servants of Christ in ministering to them. We should not come down on them harshly. They need instruction, not reproof. There is no need of "veil police" to enforce compliance in the assemblies. Our responsibility is to teach, exemplify, and encourage them to practice it.

If the elders are convinced that any sister in the assembly is "rebelling" against this practice, or divisive on this issue, let them deal with it appropriately. Such a woman also may be limited from a visible role in the assembly, if the elders feel that she is undermining the Church's position on this practice. A woman's willingness or unwillingness to wear a head covering will eventually become evident. Those who are offended by the church's stand on this issue may eventually leave that church.

2. Does the word "woman" refer only to "wife" in 1 Cor.11:3-16?

Some commentators have suggested that the "woman" in this context refers to a "wife" (English Stand Version follows this interpretation in verses that deal with head covering). The Greek word *gune* may refer to a "woman" or a "wife" depending on the context. But the whole discussion in this passage is pertaining to the headship and the creation order of *man-woman relationship in general and not just limited to husband and wife*. Paul is not dealing with a personal and family matter. The woman may be unmarried, married and in some cases her husband may not be a believer, and may not be in church. Marriage relationship is not the issue addressed here. Paul is dealing with the question of *women's* head covering, and not just *wives'* head coverings. It is applicable to any woman in Christ.

The broader view is indicated by Paul's use of "man" and woman" as opposed to "husband" and "wife." When the sense of husband and wife is intended, a pronoun is usually used ("his wife", "her husband"). Paul's arguments here are not based upon the marriage relationship. The analogy between the head covering and long hair is applicable to all women. "For as the woman originates from the man, so also the man, has his birth through the woman………" (1 Cor.11:12). This cannot mean "the husband has his birth through the wife or "born through the wife."

Paul is teaching the principle of male authority and female subordination in God-appointed relationship. The head covering is symbolizing this overall headship truth and not just a specific authority issue in one sphere. The gist of his teaching is that a woman should not disregard rules of headship. A woman's willingness to be submissive to man's authority is manifested practically in the context of relationships – a wife to her husband, a daughter to her father, or as a sister in Christ to the elders, in the church context.

The practice in some assemblies that require all girls to wear head coverings by way of encouragement (in some assemblies it seems this is even a requirement, though they may not openly admit it!) to them to understand this truth when they grow up, has no Scriptural basis. It can even degenerate into a legalistic and ritualistic practice. If a young girl chooses to wear a head covering voluntarily by recognizing the Scriptural truth it implies, it is a different matter.

3. *In which gatherings shall women cover their heads?*

In the light of Paul's teaching in 1 Cor.11, it is safe to assume that the head covering is intended in the *various gatherings of the church*. When the church assembles, as such she would cover head in recognition of her place of subjection to the authority and headship of the man, and so to Christ and God.

In 1 Cor.11:16 Paul was appealing to the practice of the *churches*. He makes no mention of the godly practice of individual sisters in Christ or any family. In other meetings (may be less formal) where saints are gathered together, it would seem appropriate that head be covered, indicating that she has not been given the authority of headship. One may also conclude with some reasonableness that *whenever* a woman assumes a public role in ministry (whether speaking *to* God or speaking *for* God) she is to wear a head covering. Thus, the principles set forth by Paul are applicable in other gatherings of the saints as well (*not by interpretation of the passage, but by application*).

If a sister believes that she should cover her head at all times of prayer including personal or family prayer, then she has the liberty to do so. But let her not try to impose her conviction on others.

One will not find too many different "meetings" In the New Testament. Some of our questions in this regard are based on the full schedule of various meetings going on almost every day in most churches today. But what we find in the New Testament is the "meeting of the church" as it was practiced by the apostles and described in the epistles (1 Cor.11-14). The practice of head covering is related to this or similar meetings.

By 'meetings of the church', I mean those gatherings where the *entire* church or corporate body is *expected* to attend (e.g. Sunday remembrance meeting, mid-week prayer meeting, etc.). The entire assembly may not be in *attendance* even at these meetings due to various reasons (e.g. travel, work, etc.), but these meetings are *intended* for all in the congregation. On the other hand, there are various meetings that are for *specific groups or purposes*, in which the *entire* assembly is *not* expected to attend/participate (e.g. Sunday school, youth meeting, ladies meeting, outreach events like VBS, etc.).

During such meetings, should the women wear a head covering? First of all, the sisters should follow whatever policy the local assembly has on this matter. If the elders in a given assembly have prayerfully decided that women should wear head coverings at ALL meetings (to avoid confusion, regardless of audience or purpose) the women should do so. If no such policy exists, then the women have freedom in this area. If a certain woman thinks she should wear a head covering at ALL meetings related to the church, let her do so. If another woman thinks she should only wear a head covering at the meetings intended for the entire body, let her practice accordingly. The one who wears a head covering at all meetings should not look down on the one who does not, and the one who only wears a head covering at certain meetings should not look down on the one who chooses to wear it all meetings.

Some wrongly interpret meetings "of the church" as "meetings in the church building". But that idea is foreign to the New Testament. If the elders have formulated a definite policy on the occasions when a woman should wear a head covering, it is good to follow that guideline for peace, order and discipline in the assembly.

4. Does 1 Cor.11:5 teach that only women who pray or prophesy (teach) must have their heads covered?

On the basis of 1 Cor.11:5, some have suggested that women could speak publicly in church meetings if their heads were covered, and that head covering applies **only** to such women who participate in public ministry. We must remember that this is not the only verse in the Bible on the subject. In **1 Cor.14:34-35 there is a clear prohibition** of women speaking in the church. The same prohibition is found again in **1 Tim.2:12,** and in **1 Tim.2:8** Paul limits public prayer in the assembly to **"the men"** (The Greek word *aner* is used here which means "men" as opposed to "women" or the "males" as opposed to "females," and not the generic word *anthropos* which would have included both sexes).

Any serious Bible student will admit the difficulty in reconciling the prohibition in 1 Cor.14:34-35 with the permission in 1 Cor.11:5. Several solutions have been suggested (a detailed interpretation of these passages are outside the scope of this book). The most satisfactory solution is to view 11:5 *not as an approval* by Paul, but only an *acknowledgment* of an **unauthorized practice** which he later corrects in 1 Cor.14. How can Paul allow in 1 Cor.11 what he prohibits in 1 Cor.14? We may also note that 1 Cor.14:34-35 is a command while 1Cor.11:5 is not a command.

In Corinth, some women were taking part in the church services with their heads uncovered. They seem to have rejected the concept of subordination. In mentioning their practice of "praying and prophesying" (this phrase may be a reference to the corporate spiritual exercise of the church when it is gathered) without head covering, Paul does not necessarily agree with it, nor is he limiting the head covering rule to women when they are actually speaking.

Dr. John Robbins' explanation in this instance is helpful:

"By here condemning the one (speaking with uncovered head) he does not commend the other (speaking).If one were to say, it is wrong to speed through a red light, he cannot be understood to say that it is right to speed. It is wrong both to speed and

178

to ignore red lights. So it is with women speaking in church uncovered. Women speaking uncovered in church is wrong, and so is women speaking in church" (Quoted by Warren Henderson, *Glories Seen and Unseen*, 114).

Warren Henderson explains that a "double error" was going on in Corinth. "Paul is simply making allusion to another abuse in the Corinthian assembly, women praying and prophesying publicly. He reproves the practice of women speaking during church meetings (i.e. while in the presence of men) in chapter 14. In lieu of confirming this practice, Paul confirmed that a "double error" was occurring in the church - unveiled women were publicly speaking in the assembly. Paul simply states that, even with the Corinthian misconception of appropriate audible ministries in the church, she ought to have had her head covered. The double error, speaking in the assembly and being uncovered, was worse than the single error of her head being covered" (*Glories Seen & Unseen*, 67).

The clear command of prohibition is given in 1 Cor.14:34-35 where Paul wholly prohibits women from speaking in the church. 1 Cor.14:34-35 is the norm and 1 Cor.11:5 must be interpreted in the light of it. Paul's subject matter in the first part of 1 Cor.11 is general issues related to headship and not speaking roles in the assembly which he addresses in detail in 1 Cor.14.

179

The pairing of *prayer* and *prophecy* demands more investigation and study. *Praying and prophesying* are typical of the prophet's activity in the Old Testament (Gen.20:7; 1 Sam.12:23; Jer.27:18; see also Luke 3:27). 1 Cor.11:5 can be a reference to *prayer associated with speaking under inspiration* (inspired utterance), a subcategory of prophesying. If so, it was a unique situation limited to the apostolic times (it must be remembered that prophecy was a temporary gift. "Prophecy" in the New Testament does not refer to simply "teaching," but to inspired utterance prompted by the Spirit of God).The present writer leans more towards this view.

Another possibility is to look at 1 Cor.11:5 as a reference to whenever and wherever it is appropriate for a woman to pray or prophesy (within the boundaries of God's Word), her deportment should reflect God's order. "Actually meetings of the assembly do not come into view until verse 17, so the instructions concerning head-covering in veres2-16 cannot be confined to church meetings. They apply to whenever a woman prays or prophesies" (William MacDonald, *Believer's Bible Commentary*, 1785). That many women have speaking gifts doesn't mean that these gifts must be exercised in a church meeting. 1 Cor.11:5 may apply to any situation where the woman assumes a position of spiritual and audible prominence.

To summarize, three possible answers (options) have been given with reference to 1 Cor.11: 5:

- Paul simply acknowledged some unauthorized practices going on in Corinth which he corrects in chapter 14.
- "Prayer" (a prophet's prayer) associated with and accompanying prophecy (inspired utterance, and not just speaking or teaching). It was a temporary gift. This was not necessarily done in the church.
- The instructions concerning head covering applies to whenever a woman prays or prophesies. In today's situation "Prophecy" may be interpreted in the general non-technical sense of "teaching," or "proclamation" of God's Word.

5. Why is head covering referred to as the "symbol of authority" (KJV: "to have power") in 1 Cor.11:10?

Symbol or sign of authority. "Symbol" is not found in the Greek text, but it is implied because of the obvious reference to the head covering in the context. It represents the universal and divine principle of headship and authority. It is a sign of sign of a woman's *submission* to the *authority* and headship of the man. This is the most natural and consistent interpretation within the context. The word "Authority" with the preposition *epi* ("over") can also be translated as "to have control over" (Mk.2:10; Luke 5:24; Rev.11:6; 20:6). In this sense, the woman is to exercise "control over" her physical head and keep it covered. This is a possible interpretation fitting to the context.

Some have construed this to mean *her* own *authority* to prophesy in the new church age or to minister under the new covenant. Still others think that the covered head represents the woman's authority or right to pray and worship, since it demonstrated her submissiveness.

"But if one is inclined to be contentious, we have no other practice, nor have the churches of God" (1 Cor.11:16)

14

Miraculous Gifts

"The signs of a true apostle were performed among you with all perseverance, by signs and wonders and miracles" (2 Cor.12:12)

Miraculous gifts are not a norm today. The more extraordinary spiritual gifts such as miracles, healings, and tongues are not essential for the normal functioning of the church. These gifts were *sign gifts*, temporary in nature used by God, primarily for confirmation and authentication of the apostolic ministry and message (2 Cor.12:12; Eph.2:20; Mark 16:20; Acts 5:12; Heb.2:3-4). The sign gifts largely passed away at the end of the apostolic era. The apostles and prophets belonged to the period of the foundation of the church (Eph.2:20). The foundation comes at the beginning and does not have to be re-laid repeatedly. Their presence and ministry in the history of the church is temporary.

It is obvious that miracles don't happen every day. On special occasions and epochs in history, God supernaturally authenticated the message and the messengers by the miracles they performed. There were three prominent periods (though miracles happened at other times) of miracles in biblical history – Moses and the Exodus, the ministries of Elijah and Elisha, and Christ and the apostle. Miracles were particularly concentrated during these eras. Miraculous phenomena were not constant in its occurrence throughout biblical history; they were actually rare. Miracles pointed to the validity both of the messenger and its message (Exodus 4:5, 31; 1 Kings 17:24; 18:36). When God's written Word was completed, methods of miraculous confirmation ceased. There was no further need for the authentication of the message. Today we believe and proclaim and already confirmed (authenticated Word). This is the general position the assemblies hold.

The Lord is sovereign. He may do whatever He pleases in heaven and on earth. The Lord may still perform miracles according to His sovereign will and pleasure and also in answer to prayer. We do recognize that a miracle or healing may be done today by God, apart from anyone's exercising a special miraculous spiritual gift. God may heal directly, through medicine, or in answer to prayer (James 5:13). It is to be noted that James does not mention about any "healers" in the church. Healing is not dependent on or effected through a specially gifted individual. From the Scriptures we also know that it is not always God's will to heal. Paul left Trophimus sick at Miletus (2 Tim.4:20). The Lord did not heal Paul of his thorn in the flesh (2 Cor.12:7-10).

The teaching in some Pentecostal/Charismatic circles that tongues are the necessary sign of having been baptized by the Holy Spirit is not scriptural. Paul said that all the believers in Corinth were baptized by the Spirit (1 Cor.12:13) but not all spoke in tongues (1 Cor.12:30).

If God wished, He could use these miraculous gifts even today. But that does not appear to be the pattern of His operations for this age. In the High priestly prayer of our Lord, His prayer went beyond the disciples even to the future generations of believers. Concerning them, the Lord said "those who believe in Me through their Word" (John 17:20). This is a reminder from the Lord that the **WORD will replace the SIGNS**.

One must also remember that the manifestation of any spiritual gift can be accepted as genuine only so far as it agrees with Scriptural teaching, and example.

Peter reminded believers to take full advantage of the divine power and promises of God, that supply an inexhaustible resource for everything pertaining to life and godliness (2 Peter 1:3 - 4). The Bible is the repository of God's precious promises that enables us to live the abundant life. Christians can enjoy an abundant Christian life and the church today can function effectively, and fulfill the Great Commission without any of the miraculous gifts.

"How shall we escape if we neglect so great a salvation? After it was at the first spoken through the Lord, it was confirmed to us by those who heard, God also bearing witness with them, both by signs and wonders and by various miracles and by gifts of the Holy Spirit according to His own will" (Heb.2:3-4).

Recommended Reading:

John MacArthur, *Charismatic Chaos*, Zondervan, 1992.

John MacArthur, *Strange Fire*, Nelson Books, 2013

Richard Gaffin, *Perspectives on Pentecost*, P&R Publishing, 1993.

Alexander Kurian, *Questions & Answers On The Gift of Tongues*, 2017.

15
Finally, Brethren

"Where there is no vision, the people perish"
(Prov.29:18, KJV)

Some may call this book a *revolutionary* book. As long as it leads to spiritual revolution in the biblical sense, I have no problem with that. My prayer is that this work should be a "biblical renewal book," challenging and motivating us to spiritual renewal. Along with an emphatic restatement and defense of the biblical distinctives we hold on to, I have humbly pointed out the areas where we need urgent and appropriate changes without biblical compromise. Simply knowing the distinctives is not the most important need for us; rather, it is necessary that we develop a proper perspective in implementing it in order to be a New Testament church in the twenty first century. Our claim on the New Testament pattern is loud and clear and we have a responsibility to prove what we claim to be. If we ignore this, what we hold on to will be a pseudo New Testament pattern. May the Lord deliver us from that peril!

We can learn valuable lessons from our own history. We should know our failures and be willing to rectify it. The state of our assemblies in many places should definitely drive us to some urgent action plans. In many assembly conferences and seminars which I have attended and ministered, there was a lot of discussion about some of these matters. But to my surprise, nothing has changed in most assemblies, and we come again the next year and discuss the same thing! Another surprise to me is that the articles and books/booklets (not many) that deal with the problems or issues we face in the assemblies always portray change *negatively* as compromise, and most of the time only highlights the unscriptural trends creeping into the assemblies. A built in parochialism and an attitude of uninformed ignorance can serve as a defense mechanism against being realistic about issues facing us today.

Any sincere appeal on Scriptural basis to evaluation, reflection, and transformation should not make us uncomfortable, but rather drive us to action. But in this book, the call to "change" is *not* a call to "compromise," or to be "trendy," or "contemporary," but to be authentically Scriptural and not slavishly follow certain things (or traditions) which we were doing for years without ever evaluating its Scriptural validity, use or relevance. Seldom have we talked about "change" *seriously*. No one wants to change the status quo. It can be risky business. But I am taking that risk for God's glory and the blessing of God's people. Change is difficult, but it is necessary. Any call for change or reform in this book is not towards New Testament principles, for it can never change. Our methods should change. We may have to reevaluate certain principles to see whether they are really New Testament principles. In truth, often a belief or practice becomes a part of our church life for pragmatic or traditional reasons, quite apart from any biblical origin. Once that happens, the search is for biblical justification and then we interpret it as a New Testament principle. This is a subtle danger.

The Word of God calls us to change − "be transformed by the renewing of your mind" (Rom.12:2). It is the transforming renewal of the mind that helps us to discern the will of God. The commitment to become "a living sacrifice" (Rom.12:1) is a commitment to change − a radical transformation, a reversal of our thinking, of our motives and methods. We have no license to alter anything which God has established for His church in His Word. The plea for change here is directed to *ourselves*. The Spirit of God will lead us through the illumination of the Word in relation to the issues and challenges dealt with in this book. We cannot continue to ignore, deny, miss or sidestep these issues any more.

In conclusion, I want to call attention again to some specific areas where we need to develop practical strategies for renewal and change based on Scriptural principles. The right pattern of gathering is not the only thing the Lord requires of us. The person of Christ and our utmost devotion to him should characterize our life and ministry. We should not love our doctrine more than we love the Lord. Our doctrine provides us the gateway to behold and comprehend the glories of our blessed Savior. With these considerations in mind, let us not fail in formulating a philosophy of ministry that is truly biblical. If we overlook these matters, it can result in great loss for us and for the next generation.

1. More emphasis and practice on positive **shepherding leadership** in the assemblies. We need people with "integrity of heart and skillfulness of hands," who can do the shepherding work as the "first priority" of their calling. Elders who are called, appointed by the Holy Spirit, gifted and able to lead the people of God; yes, a more Scriptural eldership.
2. **Elevate the quality of our pulpit/teaching/preaching ministry.** Recognize and make use of the ministry of gifted men whom God has raised in our midst. Regular, consecutive, systematic, and authoritative exposition of the Word of God should be given high priority. The traditional "hit and run" and "any man" ministry is damaging to the spiritual health of the assembly. Let us stop perpetuating the wrong practices of Word ministry in the assemblies.

3. **Be willing and open to improve the quality of the mid-week meetings**. Evaluate and review it and see if changes are necessary in relation to the day, time, schedule, format etc. Consider how it can be more beneficial to the believers. Let us do away with the mindset that "Wednesday evening" is as sacred as the doctrine of the "virgin birth."

4. Let us constantly bear in mind that **edification (building up) is the main purpose** of our spiritual exercises. Define our goals on this basis.

5. We need more **Spirit-induced vitality** and vigor in our worship meetings. This cannot be artificially implemented. Let us concentrate more on our preparation, joyful and orderly singing, and reverential attitude, appropriate and edifying sharing, broader participation etc. Unconfessed sin, monotonous routine, and legalism also can contribute to the lack of spiritual vitality. The problem of "dryness" has to be eradicated at all cost.

6. **Planning for more need-oriented and useful, edifying ministries**, seminars on missions, evangelism, spiritual leadership, and other vital issues related to faith and practice is vital; so is planning for strategically valid evangelistic outreach, prayer and preparation. Do not just ask for "volunteers" in ministries. Recognize, encourage, and enlist people in ministries according to their ability, spiritual gift, maturity

and experience. This is primarily the
responsibility of the elders.

7. "Grace and truth" should go hand in hand in our
ministries. The life of our Lord was characterized
by **"grace and truth."** We have to follow that
example. No one wants our truth without our
gracious attitude.

8. Be willing to have an open and **honest
discussion and evaluation** of our local
assemblies and its ministries. Be ready to take
the necessary action plans and implement it
under the leadership of the Holy Spirit. The
initiative for this has to come from the
leadership of the assemblies.

Let us take heed to the words of a great Brethren,
respected all over the world, H. A. Ironside:

"What is important is not 'The Brethren,' but
the truth they have.....God could set them aside, and
spread His truth by others – would I believe, though
full of gracious patience, if they be not faithful. Their
place is to remain in obscurity and devotedness, not
to think of Brethren (it is always wrong to think of
ourselves), but of souls, in Christ's name and love,
and of His glory" (*Notes on the Book of Nehemiah*,
1914, Loizeaux Brothers, 107-108).

The assemblies have been blessed by God
and have been a great influence throughout the
world. Very few Christians realize how much the

Church is indebted to the "Plymouth Brethren." We stand and build on a very noble biblical heritage. We cannot afford to weaken or dim the glories of a precious past in our generation. We believe in the power of God's Word and Spirit to reform and renew His church. It is time to change our priorities, to recognize our responsibilities, and to reaffirm our obligations. Our biblical heritage is a means to living a godly life; it provides the foundation from which we respond appropriately to God and His demands on our life. May the Lord help each one of us to "wake up and strengthen the things that remain which were about to die" (Rev.3:2).

Let us remember that the true spirit of the Brethren is REVIVAL, RENEWAL, REFORM, TRANSFORMATION, UNITY, and LOVE. This is what we need to pursue even today. May we be characterized by our renewal-revival-reformation spirit. But renewal will only come when God's people really desire it. I believe the best is yet to come!

As we live "looking for the blessed hope and glorious appearing of our great God and Savior Jesus Christ," we are encouraged to love and obey Him more and conform ourselves to His plan and purpose. May we be excited with the joy and expectations of seeing our blessed Savior, "the one who loved us and gave Himself for us." Let us do our best for Him; yes, our utmost for His highest!

The optimism of Edward Everett Hale (1822-1909), an American Unitarian minister and writer, seems to be a fitting conclusion for this book:

"I'm only one,

But I am one

I can't do everything.

But I can do something.

What I can do,

I ought to do.

And what I ought to do,

By the grace of God

I will do."

"But to this one I will look, to him who is humble and contrite of spirit, and who trembles at My word" *(Isa.66:2).*

Appendix

Frequently Asked Questions

The questions discussed here are some of the most popular and frequently asked questions the author has encountered in the past from people in the Brethren circles and also outside of it. It seems that many have received mixed messages on these issues, adding to a lot of confusion in their minds. Sometimes personal preferences and convictions on certain matters are presented from the pulpit as a part of our doctrine or distinctive. This also has contributed to the confusion in the minds of many young people. Several of these practical questions are not clearly dealt with or discussed in existing books on church doctrine and practice. Since these questions have a direct bearing on what the Brethren believe and practice, they are briefly answered here with the hope that it may be a help to all.

1. *What is the Brethren view of Bible colleges and seminaries?*

There is no official "Brethren view" on this matter. It differs from person to person or assembly to assembly. People have opinions, preferences, and convictions in relation to this question as with many other issues. But this has nothing to do with Brethren distinctives. The Brethren have Bible schools and Bible colleges in many countries of the world. Some of them offer graduate level education by faithful men committed to assembly principles and practices. In some cases, these institutions also are supported by many assemblies. Some of these teaching/training institutions have positively contributed to the growth and blessing of assemblies in certain mission fields. Most of the thriving mission fields of the Brethren have Bible training institutions.

Those who study in liberal institutions and come up with novel ideas contrary to the Scriptures are not welcomed or encouraged by the assemblies, since their teaching can negatively influence believers. This is true of all conservative evangelical churches. Assemblies do not *require* a seminary degree or special theological training for ministry, though this can be helpful to one's ministry. Many assemblies are now recognizing the value of some kind of formal biblical education for Christian workers.

A minority of the Brethren are opposed to formal theological education and theological institutions. They may have "their own reasons" for it. It is ironic to find that these men, who eschew all formal training, read and study from the writings of seminary professors and other formally trained men. In their legalistic rigidity, they find no problem in reading, studying, and profiting from them in their private study, but they are against listening to them in a classroom??

Most of the early Brethren were all well educated and formally trained men. Even in our generation, we have been blessed through the ministry of academically trained servants of God in our assemblies, world over. Since most assemblies are not able to provide good and systematic training in the Word, formal training is a legitimate option for those who desire it, provided such training upholds the inspiration and authority of the Word of God, and the training is done under godly men. It is a biblical truth that the Holy Spirit uses human means to teach and prepare others.

2. Do the Brethren have an official position on para-church organizations?

As far as para church organizations are concerned, the assemblies have no official position. In the light of the New Testament ecclesiology (doctrine of the Church) the assemblies believe that the priority is always for the church and its ministries, and not for para church organizations. But we are not against para church ministries. Many para-church agencies are doing commendable jobs in translating the Bible, propagating the Gospel, in training ministries, and in reaching out to a lost world. Their contributions should not be minimized. Many honorable Brethren also are serving in such organizations. It is always desirable that the para-church agencies help the work of the local churches, rather than hinder it. In many countries, there are several Brethren para-church ministries supported by the local assemblies.

3. Is it acceptable for a person in a Brethren church to listen to messages by non-Brethren preachers, read books by non-Brethren authors, or attend non-Brethren conferences/training?

The Brethren are not sectarian. Most of us listen to other good evangelical preachers, teachers and theologians, and also profit from their writings. We honor and value the spiritual contribution of all those who belong to the body of Christ, as long as it is in accordance with the truth of Scriptures. We share the fundamentals of the faith with the evangelicals at large.

Like in other areas of faith, some believers, on the basis of personal reasons or convictions, may not listen to other (non-Brethren) preachers or read other authors. I also have come across some very devoted fellow-Brethren who do not read anything other than the Bible. That is a personal matter. But when such matters are voiced from the pulpit as doctrine or imposed upon others as a golden rule for Christian life, we have to reject it. If we hear such opinions, it has nothing to do with the "Brethren" as such.

When we listen to others and try to learn from their teachings, we have to make sure that they are sound in doctrine and practice. This is true even when we listen to Brethren preachers and teachers also. If we are not quite sure of the doctrinal soundness of some authors or preachers, it is better to ask others who are mature and knowledgeable in these matters. Even when one attends a conference or a training program conducted by "others", we have to make sure that it is done in a way that honors the Lord and is faithful to His Word. If certain things which they teach or promote are against one's personal convictions, we have the freedom to reject it. We don't have to "buy it all."

Discernment is very important in these decisions. It is always better to keep away from any preacher (e.g. many TV preachers) who have the slogan "God told me to tell you," or "I had this vision last night." Hold on to your wallet and run. Their tricky methods, manipulative techniques, and false teachings are contrary to the Scriptures and we have to reject them. Many mega-church pastors who do not preach the Gospel are also to be rejected. The message of the Gospel that is to be proclaimed to the nations is clearly defined by the Lord in Luke's version of the Great Commission. "Repentance for forgiveness of sins should be proclaimed in His name to all the nations" (Luke 24:47). Those who do not preach "grace," "faith," "repentance" and "sin" do not deserve our attention, however motivational or influential they may be. So we have to apply some Scriptural yardsticks in these decisions.

We have a responsibility to provide systematic teaching and training within the assemblies. Many of the assembly believers tend to go to non-assembly settings, because some of these much needed spiritual resources are not available in their local assemblies. We are in shortage of visionary leadership who are burdened about these matters and who are willing to plan strategic ministries for the growth and equipping of believers.

4. *In connection with the previous question, is there anything wrong if a Brethren assembly decides to follow/study a book by a non-Brethren author, as an aid to Bible study (provided, of course, that the book does not contradict the Scriptures)? For example, if a young couples group in an assembly is looking for a study guide on marriage/family, should they first look for something by a 'Brethren author'?*

There is nothing wrong in studying a book by non-brethren in the church or groups as long as it is scripturally sound. It may be a good idea to take opinions from people knowledgeable on books and authors. In certain cases, we may have to be discerning about some particular chapters or sections in the book (this can be true even for Brethren authors!). All the Bible translations we use (except for the JN Darby translation), many song books, VBS and evangelism tools, theology books and commentaries, etc., are written by non-Brethren people.

5. *Most Brethren churches are smaller in size compared to many other denominations. Is having a 'small' church a Brethren Distinctive?*

A small church is not a Brethren distinctive, but rather a Brethren *preference* for *practical* reasons. For more meaningful participation in the "open worship," for more people to exercise their spiritual gifts in the assembly meetings, and for the enjoyment of close-knit fellowship, the Brethren have always encouraged small churches (a particular number as an ideal number cannot be specified). But this concept is not welcomed by all Brethren.

But some Brethren stretch this preference to an undue proportion and make a false doctrine out of it. This creates confusion. By becoming "too small" some assemblies find it very difficult to survive. Actually, God is not opposed to numbers in the church. Throughout the Book of Acts, Luke peppers his historical account of the early church with report of church growth. At least 17 times, the Holy Spirit calls our attention to the numerical growth of the Church in Acts. The first church established in Jerusalem was a mega-church (of course, very different in doctrine and practice from many of the mega-churches of our time). We find large churches in the Bible and also in church history.

A large church may have advantages and disadvantages. This can be true of a small church also. A growing church is not injurious to church health; neither does it have to be a compromised church. There is unmistakable emphasis in the book of Acts both on *quantitative and qualitative* church growth. There are some large Brethren churches in many countries of the world doing commendable service in the name of the Lord and for His glory. We are not hostile or opposed to large churches if the Lord enlarges the borders of those gatherings. We must welcome whatever the Lord does with His church.

6. Can a Brethren believer attend a non-Brethren church if one happens to find himself/herself in a place where there is no Brethren church nearby?

Many young people from Brethren assemblies and families are attending non-Brethren churches today, even in places where there are Brethren assemblies. They may have their own reasons for it. The question here is about an exceptional situation. Yes, in such situations one may look for a good Bible-believing, Christ-honoring, and Gospel-preaching church as the next option. After all, finding a local church and making it one's home-church is a personal responsibility, based on one's doctrinal understanding and personal convictions.

We understand that there are some gatherings of God's people holding on to the truth of God's Word, although they do not openly identify with the Brethren assemblies.

7. Many Brethren churches do not officially recognize various Christian holidays, such as Christmas or Easter. Is there a Scriptural reason for this? Is it wrong to celebrate/recognize such holidays as a church?

Some of the contemporary practices in Christian celebrations have pagan origins. Though Christmas and Easter are based on historical events, the exact day or date is not known. These celebrations are commemorated mainly on the basis of traditions. True and false elements have crept into them. The greedy business world and the biblically ignorant Christians have commercialized these events. There is no command for believers to observe or celebrate these events. There is nothing in the Word which *requires* a Christian to observe Christmas or Easter. We give importance to observe things that the Lord and the apostles taught and commanded us in the Word to remember and to celebrate. Other than this basic position, I don't think the Brethren have an official position on these matters.

I personally do not believe it is sinful to celebrate Christmas, to a degree, any more than it would be sinful to celebrate the birthday of a family member. But we should not celebrate anything in a sinful way. From a practical and evangelistic standpoint, these major Christian events/holidays bring lot of opportunities to share the Gospel with others through hospitality, carol singing, or special house meetings by inviting friends. It may be even a good idea to conduct special programs in the churches. Many people, who may not be open to Christian meetings or messages, may be open on these special days when invited by their friends. This has been proved true on a number of occasions. Even when the world "wrongly" celebrates these events, as believers, we can meaningfully reflect upon these great events in the salvation history and thank and worship our God. Even studying and preaching on these great truths during the season can be very refreshing and spiritually revitalizing. We can make such meaningful celebrations that are spiritually stimulating and edifying.

Let us allow those who choose to celebrate it appropriately the freedom to do so, and not try to bring in legalistic ideologies in relation to these matters so as to give them a "Brethren" color. Whether or not a church 'officially' recognizes days such as Christmas or Easter will be up to the leadership of each local church to decide. Let them celebrate or not celebrate. That is their prerogative. There is no official Brethren position or policy on such things. Each assembly is autonomous and independent.

8. Is not using musical instruments during the worship/remembrance meeting, and in general, singing more hymns than choruses at all meetings, a Brethren Distinctive?

The non-use of musical instruments in worship service in the assemblies is based more on *practical* reasons than doctrinal reasons. The Brethren consider the Lord's Supper meeting as the most important meeting of the church. Hence, all the Brethren churches try to maintain a sacred solemnity to the occasion. Musical instruments during this time can become a distraction and take away our focus from the center of our worship. The spirit of worship can be hindered by the show of the musical talents of the players. Since a special significance is attached to the worship and remembrance, traditionally most Brethren assemblies do not like to have musical instruments during this time. It is more a matter of preference than doctrine.

Of course, the above arguments are not infallible; they may be challenged. Many assemblies now use organ or piano during the worship time. Some have even turned to the use of other musical instruments. Let them decide whether it is a help or hindrance. These matters should not be considered as part of the distinctive.

I do not know how the attitude of "no instruments whatsoever at any time in the assembly" can be justified in any way. That may be the preference of some Brethren. Sometimes such extreme policies stem out of legalistic rigidity. They are free to maintain it. But it is dangerous when they make it a doctrine and try to impose it on others.

The Brethren are not against musical instruments. But it's appropriate and dignified use according to occasions is emphasized in the assemblies. One has to be very cautious about the popular concept in many charismatic and evangelical churches that worship is *predominantly* related to music and it is music driven. In this concept "praise and worship" is mainly a music performance by a "worship team." This is false theology. Brethren assemblies are not sympathetic or supportive of such theologically false approaches to worship.

As far as hymns and choruses are concerned, the Brethren assemblies do not have a uniform policy. Most believers in the older generation are used to singing more hymns than choruses. So they maintain that preference and it has to be honored. But it will be good if they are also sensitive to the needs of the young generation and allow choruses and contemporary songs that are scripturally sound. The question should not be whether it is new or old, or hymns or choruses. The primary question has to do with the lyrics. Are the words scripturally and doctrinally sound?

The rigid policy of using just one particular hymn book alone may not be very helpful today. Old hymnbooks are good and very helpful. Great hymns of the faith have never been replaced by modern songs. But we should also be willing to accommodate other doctrinally sound song books in the assemblies. One has to be very careful about the many ego-centric choruses celebrating a kind of "eros" spirituality and "falling in love" with God. Our "love songs" in worship must be characterized by adoring love and not sentimental love. To have a healthy policy in relation to songs in the assembly is a great need. We have to pick and choose in this process considering the young and old in the assemblies.

Generally speaking, the Brethren encourage congregational singing in the gathering of the church.

9. Is not wearing jewelry by some Brethren believers from India a Brethren distinctive?

This is a very frequently asked question by many young people who grew up in the Indian assemblies (hence the question and its answer may not be relevant to many of my readers). *This is not a Brethren distinctive at all.* A distinctive has to be biblically and doctrinally based. Since the vast majority of the Brethren around the world use some sort of jewelry, it is clear proof that not using jewelry has no biblical basis. Even in India, this is mainly (or only) restricted to the Brethren and Indian Pentecostal Churches of the state of Kerala.

The Brethren movement in Kerala was a very powerful revival and separatist movement. Most of the early Brethren in Kerala came out of large denominational churches, and some even from wealthy and high caste families. Silver and gold were their social status symbols. Giving gold also was a part of dowry. When people from these denominational families embraced a new faith, they were persecuted and stripped of all their wealth and family inheritance. But these heroes of faith "considered the reproach of Christ greater riches than the treasures of Egypt."

To demonstrate the vitality of their faith and witness, they willingly and happily renounced many things in life. *Jewelry was only one among them.* They also practiced simple life style with no luxury, did not do any work on the Lord's day, had no interest in amassing wealth or a big bank balance, would never miss a worship meeting (some of them used to say "If you are not dead, you have to be at the worship meeting"), did not allow children to study school lessons on Saturday evenings (since it was considered to be a preparation time for the Lord's day), preferred simple/white clothes etc.

All these things were done in sincerity to show their consecration to the things of the Lord, and also as a testimony before the world. They also considered these practices as symbols of their "separation" from the world. What is important to the world was not important to them. They wanted to be "different" from the denominational church goers. This also helped to abolish the social distinction within the church between the rich (jewelry wearers) and poor (non-jewelry wearers). **But none of these things were a part of the "doctrine"**; they were noble practices for valid reasons. These practices were followed willingly and voluntarily out of personal conviction.

It is true that some over-zealous souls eventually placed the "jewelry issue" on a par with doctrine or rather confused it with doctrine through over emphasis (since non-use of jewelry was considered the most obvious trait of separation). Many believers still value these noble traditions and are committed to it as personal preference, and not as a doctrine. Many others are trapped by the spirit of legalism and made the jewelry issue a 'sort of doctrine' and try to impose it on others. They become very judgmental on all Christians who use jewelry and consider it as even "unspiritual." It is sad and even a shame to say that removal of jewelry is required in some assemblies (only a minority) to be welcomed to the Lord's Supper, or even to get baptized. Unbelievable, but it is true! What a departure from the truth of God's Word! Since this is a very "sensitive" issue in many places, even many Bible teachers and preachers keep silent about it, though they are fully aware of the unscriptural nature of this grossly legalistic stand.

It is rather amusing to note that those who still insist on the non-use of jewelry have embraced a "theology of convenience." They have rejected all the other noble practices of the "fathers" in relation to wealth, luxury, simple life-style, working on Sundays, Saturday evening devoted to preparation for Sunday etc. But they still concentrate on one thing – jewelry!

Legalism among God's people is a common problem all over the world. We must avoid elitism, legalism, libertinism and judgmentalism in these matters. We should not be obsessed with material things. Do not look down on those who are convinced to lead their Christian lives with or without jewelry, but make sure you know that this is *not* a Brethren distinctive, rather, a part of a noble Kerala Brethren tradition. But unfortunately some legalists have portrayed this as a doctrine.

10. *Even though we do not believe in fundraising, is there anything wrong with making financial needs for Christian ministries known? What about financial needs of evangelists in the mission fields (e.g. needs for hospital bills or children's education, marriage, etc)? What is the best way to make these needs known?*

There is nothing wrong in making legitimate financial needs known to others (e.g. needs of evangelists or missionaries in the mission field). After all, if information is not given, how are people supposed to know what the needs are? People may use various methods to make their needs known if they prefer to do this. There are many among the Brethren who out of personal conviction and policy do not even mention, share or publish their personal or ministry related need. I was raised in a home where this conviction was followed, taught and exemplified and this has gone deep into my life and ministry. This does not mean that all Brethren think alike in this matter. It is difficult to say what the best method of communicating the need is. Some may personally communicate; others may do it with the help of the local assembly/ elders for more credibility, if this is possible.

Traditionally, Brethren do not practice raising funds (though this is changing), but neither do we condemn people for doing it in an honest way for genuine needs. We should also note that there is a difference between giving information (making needs known) and 'fundraising' (often forcing/ manipulating/compelling people to give). Christian giving is always willing, voluntary and cheerful giving through the exercise in the heart by the Spirit of God. Brethren are "big" on this solid scriptural principle.

The Brethren don't have a "doctrine" in relation to making needs known or fund raising etc., but our position is more of a practice based on the principle of faith and the apostolic precedent. The great heroes of faith like George Muller and Anthony Norris Groves are great inspiration to many Brethren even today.

The modern practice of sending bank details with emails and financial appeals, or purposely visiting assemblies or families with the sole intention of collecting money (e.g. for a hall construction) are all a *kind of fund raising,* even though we may not use that term! Let each one judge on its merits or demerits.

11. Suppose a local assembly decides to regularly give a full time worker in their midst a FIXED amount of money, not as a 'condition of employment' or at the demand of the worker, but out of the assembly's goodwill and desire to meet the needs of the worker and his family. Is there anything unscriptural about this?

There is nothing unscriptural about this. Some would say that support is fine, but if it is a fixed amount, it is wrong (since it could be seen as a 'salary'). But the issue should not be whether it is a *fixed* amount or *different* amount each time; the issue is whether it goes against biblical principles. The distinction between a 'fixed' amount and 'different' amount is one in our mind; the Scripture makes no distinction regarding amount. In fact, it is silent regarding the amount! Sometimes, we have unnecessarily developed our own 'taboo' to some of these things, just to be different from others without any valid reasons. The Word of God clearly teaches that the Lord's work and workers are to be supported by the Lord's people (1 Cor.9:11, 14; 1 Tim.5:17-18; Gal.6:6). This responsibility should not be overlooked on the basis of some "pet ideas" which we have cherished for years. We have to be systematic, regular and practical in our giving and support of the Lord's workers. Whatever methodology we may choose has to be "realistic."

12. *There is often a complaint that Brethren assembly meetings are 'dry' and that as Brethren, we generally shy away from showing much emotion, raising/clapping our hands, or saying 'Hallelujah' in our meetings, like some other Christian groups do. Is this one of our distinctives?*

This has nothing to do with our distinctives. Some of these things may be true of some assemblies in the West. Many Brethren assemblies Asia and most of Africa, Mexico and South America are very vibrant in their singing with clapping hands and really expressing the joy of the Lord in the worship. Some of these things may be cultural also. Lack of vitality has been a complaint against the Brethren assemblies even by many Brethren themselves.

I believe liveliness should characterize our worship and ministry. This is an area where we need more attention. Many assemblies struggle with deadness. In some cases, this may be an overreaction to the wrong practices of the Charismatics. One must remember that it is not a *necessity* to say "Hallelujah" in the gathering of the church. Though worship is not emotional, there is an aspect in worship where emotion under the control of the Holy Spirit also has a part. In the book of Psalms, the three key elements of worship are *Experience, Emotion and Expression.* Worship in spirit and in truth is not against this concept. Assemblies who feel this deficiency should prayerfully consider ways through which they can improve on this.

13. Is it acceptable for a Brethren church to cooperate with another church (non-Brethren) for some activity? For example, if an evangelical, Bible believing church in the neighborhood approaches us and asks for our help in an upcoming outreach event, what should our approach/attitude be?

We are not against cooperating with other conservative evangelical churches if that is necessary. One of our distinctives is that we are non-sectarian and we uphold the unity of the Body of Christ. But unfortunately, this is only in theory, at least in the case of most assemblies. In various mission fields around the world, assemblies cooperate with other evangelical bodies, especially for the preaching of the Gospel, VBS, and other outreach events. Such cooperation, if it is needed, should be planned by the elders with care and discernment. It is left to each local assembly to make this decision. If any assembly thinks that it is not in their best interest to have such cooperation, they don't have to go for it. Openness for cooperation with other Christians is definitely a Brethren trait.

14. What is the scope of silence regarding women in the assembly (1 Cor.14:34)? Does it include all forms of speaking or even singing? Are there occasions when it is permissible for women to speak in the church?

I believe the prohibition in 1 Cor.14:34 include all forms of public speaking in the assembly (in the formal gathering of the church for worship, prayer, exercise of spiritual gifts, and teaching of the Word of God).

Paul spells out three regulations for the church meetings in 1 Cor.14:26-40:

1. Regulations on speaking in tongues (14:27-28).
2. Restrictions on prophecy (14:29-30).
3. Prohibition on women's public speaking (14:34-35).

There is nothing ambiguous about these regulations. The third command (verses 34-35) is as clear and conclusive as the other two in the chapter. The command seems very clear: women are not to do any public speaking in the church. In the light of 1 Tim 2:11-12 the prohibition particularly refers to the official speaking in the capacity of preaching, teaching or giving authoritative instruction.

The most popular view in recent years on the prohibition on women's speaking in the church, is to limit the prohibition only to the "judging" or "evaluating" (NIV: "weighing") prophesies 14:29 . But the prohibition is directly related to "speaking," and not just one form of speaking, i.e. the evaluation of prophecy. As Paul instructed tongue-speakers and prophets to be "silent" in verses 28, and 30, in verse 34 he instructs women to be "silent." As Paul, instructed tongue-speakers and prophets about their "speaking" (14:27, 29), in verse 34 he instructs women also about their "speaking" in the church. The verb "to speak" here cannot be restricted to or limited to speak in a certain manner or on a certain topic. Women are not to do any public speaking in the church. The statement leaves no question as to its meaning. They are to receive instruction with entire submissiveness (1 Tim.2:11), and "if they desire to learn anything, let them ask their own husbands at home" (1 Cor.14:35).

The prohibition does not include singing. In Eph.5:19 and Col.3:16 the whole company of believers join in the singing to mutual edification and instruction. Congregational singing is only a *participatory* role. Moreover, *the verb "speak" does not refer to singing.* Believers in church gatherings represent the body of Christ. Those who speak or

217

lead (even leading in prayer) are in *de facto* leadership roles.

If an assembly has a policy where women may share testimony or reports of various ministries in which they are involved in, or share a prayer request in the meeting of the church, I will leave that as the responsible decision of the leadership of the assembly and will not quarrel with them on these matters. But be aware of the fact that someone can exhort, teach and instruct even through a testimony.

15. What does "exercise authority over a man" in 1 Tim. 2:12 refer to? Are there any leadership positions a woman may occupy in a church?

"But I do not allow a woman to teach or exercise authority over a man." I go with the plain meaning of what it says: women must not have dominion over a man or exercise authority over a man. In the context, it may even refer to usurping the authority of male leaders or teachers in the church. Another popular interpretation is that women may exercise their spiritual gifts in a variety of ministries in a local assembly, as long as those gifts are exercised under the leadership of men (elders). Though this is a general principle, this meaning seems odd here in the context and it tries to twist what is obvious.

1 Tim.2:11-12 clearly prohibits women from offices of leadership and public teaching in the

assembly. According to Greek grammarians the present infinitive form *didaskein* in 2:12 ("to teach") would be best translated "to be a teacher" ("I do not permit a woman to be a teacher"). Women may teach in ministries and forums that are particularly suited for them within the boundaries of God's Word, as long as they do not usurp the place of leadership and authority of men in the church. Paul himself declares that women can teach other women and children (Titus 2:3-4; 2 Tim.3:14-15).There may be certain situations in which it may be difficult to decide whether a woman's participation may infringe any of these guidelines. In such situations, the policy formulated by the elders should be followed.

A woman may occupy leadership positions in relation to women's ministry and children's ministry, or other appropriate ministries within the Scriptural guidelines mentioned earlier.

CPSIA information can be obtained
at www.ICGtesting.com
Printed in the USA
LVHW030915140321
681500LV00007B/470